THEY FINISHED THEIR COURSE IN
THE EIGHTIES

THEY FINISHED THEIR COURSE IN THE EIGHTIES

Compiled by
JAMES ANDERSON

© J. Ritchie Ltd. 1990

Published by John Ritchie Ltd.
40 Beansburn
Kilmarnock
Ayrshire KA3 1RH

ISBN 0 946351 22 8

Printed in Scotland by
Bell and Bain Ltd., Glasgow

CONTENTS

INTRODUCTION ix
ERIC BARKER 1
R. W. BEALES OF IPSWICH 5
ARCHIE H. BOULTON 11
Dr. JOHN BOYD 15
JOHN BRITTON. 19
ARTHUR JAMES CHILCOTT 23
WILLIAM HENRY CLARE 29
JIMMY CUTHBERTSON 33
H. L. ELLISON 39
ALBERT FALLAIZE 43
JOHN FISKE 51
ANDREW GRAY 55
GEORGE HARPUR 59
JEFFREY HARRISON 63
STUART HINE & ALEC McGREGOR 67
HOWARD HITCHCOCK 77
G. C. D. HOWLEY 83
ERIC HUTCHINGS 87
MARK KAGAN 91
ALBERT LECKIE 97
Dr. GEORGE McDONALD 103
TOM McKELVEY 109
CHARLES MARSH 113
HEDLEY GLOVER MURPHY 119
A. NAISMITH & W. F. NAISMITH 125
CHARLES OXLEY 135
A. E. PHILLIPS 139
ARNOLD PICKERING 143
ALEC PULLENG 147

TOM REA 153
DUNCAN REID. 157
WILLIE REW 163
JOHN R. ROLLO 169
JOHN RUDDOCK 173
RALPH SHALLIS 177
JAMES M. S. TAIT 183
F. A. TATFORD. 187
FRED WHITMORE 193
HAROLD WILDISH 197
DAVID WILLCOX 203
R. J. WRIGHT 209
ELLIS HARRISON 217
CONCLUSION—THE QUIET MAJORITY . . . 221

PUBLISHERS' PREFACE

It is with a real sense of loss that we record the service and labours of some of the Lord's servants who were called home in the last decade. And yet it is with deep thanksgiving to God that we can truly state that "they finished their course".

Nothing more can be added to the work which these dear servants have done—their record is on high. Yet something can be built on their accomplishments and devotion to their Lord. It is the desire of the Publishers that this volume, which can only really give a very brief account of what has been done, may inspire its readers to emulate these men of God, and that there may be those raised by God Himself who will fill the ranks of the Faithful who have rested from their labours.

Our appreciation must be expressed to Mr. J. Anderson for his diligent and painstaking work in the compilation of this book, and to all who furnished details which helped him to compile this second volume as a worthy addition to his earlier work, on those servants of the Lord who finished their course in the Seventies.

Kilmarnock, October 1990   THE PUBLISHERS.

INTRODUCTION

It is now over ten years since the first little volume entitled "They Finished Their Course" was published. That volume was sold out in less than a year and its reception and further requests for that kind of thing made it desirable that what was done for outstanding brethren who finished their course in the seventies should be done for those who were called home in the eighties.

Missionaries play a larger part in this volume than they did in the last, but that is so because such a large number of amazing missionaries finished their course in the eighties. Anne Arnot who left assemblies claimed that many of our best people went to the mission field. The worth of those whose stories are told here is incalculable on this side of the glory. Nor does this book tell the whole story. Naturally we expect our readership to be drawn from our side of the Atlantic, but it was tempting to include the stories of some who belonged to the U.K. but whose later domicile was across the Ocean.

I refer to Adam Ferguson of Edinburgh who married in America and who did a magnificent job in South Africa. Some of his contemporaries as young Christians still survive and would have loved his story to be told. I refer to Sydney Saword of Venezuela, another long liver, who originated in Southend in Essex, and who served the Lord for seventy years in Venezuela, and whose family to the third generation are serving the same Lord in Central America. I refer to Dr. Tidmarsh, commended from England in 1939, who did a great translation project in Ecuador, and to Cyril Brooks of Surrey, almost the father of assembly missionary work in the Philippines, several members of whose family are carrying it on. Where was the line to be drawn? In a book like this we are not scraping the bottom of the barrel, but skimming the surface of the great story of the assemblies' contribution to world evangelisation, coupled with Bible translation, often involving reducing a language to writing before the translations could proceed.

And one of the amazing facts about quite a number of these men is their longevity. Two centenarians figure in this book, ten nonagenarians and thirteen in their eighties. All of this in spite of the hard lives which some of them lived. What a tribute to the preservative grace of God! They may have endured hardness as good soldiers of Jesus Christ, but they didn't abuse their bodies as many a worldling does.

This exercise was not just to unearth history although it did just that. It wasn't to idolise men or create heroes of them. It was to focus attention on our heritage. It was to fire our zeal. It was to highlight men who refused to say no. They battled through unimaginable difficulties. Even in the face of closed doors, and after retirement they were still finding ways of serving God. If we were all to show the same spirit assemblies wouldn't be in the doldrums, and the Lord's work wouldn't be languishing.

Another feature of some of the men whose stories figure here is that they were men of principle. Assembly principles were held dear by most of them. Others had strong objections to military service and paid a price for doing so. One felt deeply about the desecration of the Lord's Day and did something about it. Another fought heroically against the moral evils of our society. Do we do enough in the fight against evil?

Once again I must apologise to our sisters. Nearly all of the men who are featured here had wives who stood in the battle with them. Among my saddest memories are those of men who led assemblies and who made shipwreck after their wives died. This simply illustrated how much those men depended on their wives. How could the men of this book have done what they did without their's? Sisters, you are saluted for the backing you give, for the relief you provide from family responsibilities, for the hardships you accept in the cause of the gospel.

And now a big thank you to all who furnished information for the stories told here. Some of you entered into the exercise with great gusto. Some of you ransacked files to unearth memories—and photos. This kind of book requires a lot of teamwork. Thanks for being one of the team.

I trust that you are not too disappointed if somebody you esteemed isn't included here. The selection is quite arbitrary. I had an acquaintance of different degrees with all but a dozen of those who figure in my book. No doubt this influenced my choice. Nor should I forget to point out that there were people who didn't respond to the invitation to contribute. It was Job who said, "My record is on high". (Job 16:19).

Finally, we come to those who are not likely to be mentioned in human dispatches like this, the unknown warriors. J. R. Cochrane of the U.S.A. and the Dominican Republic, wrote a biography in Spanish of one of those great missionaries mentioned in this book, Duncan Reid. He also wrote an article for the American missionary magazine, "Missions", entitled "The Quiet Majority", with sub-title, "The Unsung Heroes of the Church". I have taken the liberty of taking excerpts from that article. At the end of the day "the righteous Judge" will give the crowns, and the cities, to those to whom they rightly belong. Meantime, "Keep the bright reward in view".

James Anderson

ERIC BARKER
(1899–1989)

ERIC BARKER

Eric had the distinction of having a father and a grandfather who were full time in the Lord's service before he was. His grandfather, William, edited a publication called, "Simple Testimony", and was the author of "Twelve Bible Dialogues"— hardly what we would expect from modern Exclusives. William's son, Harold P. Barker was too interested in the salvation of the lost to remain in that fellowship, and, on leaving it he wrote a pamphlet entitled, "Why I Abandoned Exclusivism". Thereafter he became a well-known evangelist, missionary and Bible teacher among Open assemblies, his ministry extending to several continents.

It was in this man's home that Eric Barker grew up. It was he who first interested his son in missionary work. Young Eric was just nine when he was saved, like many another youngster from an assembly home, because every latecoming home from an assembly meeting, was feared to be because the Lord had come and the parents had been raptured, and the children left behind for judgement.

When Eric was sixteen his father asked him what he would like to be in life. The youngster's reply included becoming a missionary, a sailor and a banker. In fact Eric Barker experienced all three. Leaving school he took up employment in a bank. To meet the requirements of National Service he became a sailor. He returned to the bank after World War One, but within a few years he became a missionary. Before going off to sea, Eric had commenced serving the Lord—in the Sunday School in Bermondsey, in Model Lodging Houses in London, and in open air work.

In his travels H. P. Barker visited Spain and Portugal and came home to describe the very great spiritual darkness in those

1

very Catholic countries. The outcome was that Herbert Biffen went to Spain for almost the rest of his life, while Eric Barker went to Portugal.

First, Eric joined a Portuguese brother who had recently given up his secular employment in order to serve the Lord—Sr. Jose Freire. Together they covered many miles of the country distributing tracts and selling scriptures from a two-wheeled, mule cart. Then Eric was called to a place in North Portugal where a work was in danger of dying because of the serious illness of an aged Portuguese brother. Eric rented a house there until he came home in 1922. Returning home in 1922 Eric got married, taking his wife back to Portugal to resume his mule-cart work. Together they took the scriptures to the crowds attending all the fairs of the area and saw many places opened up to the gospel.

A growing family made a difference to Eric's circumstances. The city of Oporto had an English school for his children and the city provided him with employment, by means of which he supported himself and his children. His commending assembly had never promised financial support so, like Paul before him, Eric engaged in tent-making. However he continued living in Cacia and serving the Lord there, travelling daily to work in Oporto until somebody else arrived to relieve him.

Then the Barkers purchased a property in Oporto which was to serve as their home and hall. Here Sunday afternoons were spent at open air meetings outside the railway stations, resulting in a number of conversions and another hall being obtained at Valvadores. But World War Two broke out and the British Government advised all of their citizens to return home as Hitler was in danger of overrunning the whole of Europe. The Barkers had already lost one son with peritonitis; they were now to lose the rest of their family. The ship bringing them home was torpedoed and only the captain and the crewmen who were on deck when the torpedo struck were saved. Those who perished in the disaster included Mrs. Barker and seven children, and her father, Eric's sister and her three daughters, and another missionary couple and their two children. In all Eric Barker lost fourteen relatives in that dreadful disaster. In reply to a comforter, he wrote, "I had been telling the Lord very much of late that all I had was His, and He took me at my word. Now He is saying to me, "My grace is sufficient for thee and I'm trying to take Him at His word".

When Eric's employer heard of the disaster he gave him a fortnight's holiday to recover from the shock, but Eric went off to Lisbon and preached every night in crowded halls in which many were saved. Five years later he met Miss Beryl Scott and family life recommenced. The rest of their lives were to be given to the Lord's work in Oporto. Eric was both an evangelist and a Bible teacher and for this last reason was in great demand. Our European missionaries of the "old brigade" seldom came home so that we didn't get to know their value in preaching and teaching. Latterly his health was poor and it was the intention to bring him home, but a rapid deterioration hindered such an intention being fulfilled so that Eric Barker's burial took place in his beloved Portugal and his funeral was attended by many whom he had pointed to the Saviour. He was within sight of having served the Lord in Portugal for seventy years.

A series of articles about Eric were produced by Paulo Pina Leile and published in the Portuguese magazine. The information in them was collected from all over Portugal.

R. W. BEALES OF IPSWICH
(1895–1983)

R. W. BEALES

Reginald Woodhouse Beales born into a Methodist family in Norwich where the family remained until he had left school and found a job in a solicitor's office. However his family then moved to Ipswich where he obtained a job in an architect's office which set him off on his professional career.

World War One commenced and like other young men Reg. Beales was called up, joining the R.A.M.C. Here he found himself among a remarkable group of young Christians—a doctor, a medical student, a solicitor, a shoemaker, a postmaster, an engineer, all of whom were to be Christian leaders in their own right in the post-war period. Presumably the engineer, to whom I am indebted for my information, was John Harry Brown, who at 90 plus is still serving the Lord in Africa. It was while he was with this crowd that Reg. Beales' spiritual history began.

Frank Murton of Norwich preached to him while they were on the march, as the result of which he got saved. When Harry Brown joined the company in Blackpool Reg. was unbaptised and just a babe in Christ. When he was ready for baptism various obstacles had to be overcome. First the small local assembly only met once per week because of the black-out. However they loaned the Gospel Hall to the young soldiers for Reg.'s baptism. The tank was very shallow, Reg. was rather tall, and none of the young soldiers had ever baptised anybody before. The Scottish solicitor was the eldest of the young soldiers so he was chosen to be the baptiser and he had problems getting Reg. truly buried. Harry Brown wrote, "In picture form it really was the end of Reg. Beales naturally, because from them on he made rapid progress."

(It is worth mentioning for the record that Frank Murton who preached to Reg. Beales on route marches later commenced a

5

work at Cortessey, near Norwich by staging a Sunday School in his garage, and then building a Gospel Hall in his garden. Today a large new hall exists in memory of Mr. & Mrs. Murton, and there is a thriving assembly).

Following their training that group of young Christian soldiers were scattered abroad on active service, Reg. Beales being sent to India and Persia. During his time abroad he learned one or two Indian languages, hoping to return as a missionary. He was never able to do this, but he had a lifelong missionary interest. Until a few weeks of his homecall he kept in touch with Harry Brown during his long life of missionary service in Zaire and S. Africa. Many missionaries from various parts of the world stayed in the family home and left impressions on the young folk. And if he never went to India as a missionary he was able to write articles for an Indian magazine, "The Christian Steward." Back home Reg. recommenced his architectural work. He obtained his qualifications while in employment and set up his own practice in Ipswich in his own house in 1926, transferring later to office premises in the city. His business was successful so much so that at one time there was a family proposal to draw a map of Ipswich pinpointing the houses, shops, etc., that he had designed. In addition he was responsible for drawing the plans for many Gospel Halls throughout East Anglia. As a successful architect he was able to help Christians with accommodation and materially.

Following the First World War Mr. Beales spent some of his holidays helping evangelists James Ashby and Charles Wyncoll in tent work in Norfolk and Suffolk. It is suggested that Mr. Wyncoll, Counties Evangelist for Suffolk was invited outside of that county for meetings and that Mr. Beales took his place. Thus started work at the Great Wenham with which his name is always associated, and in which he engaged until the outbreak of World War Two. At first the meetings were held in a garage in Capel St. Mary, an adjoining village with the gospel work being conducted in a disused railway carriage at Great Wenham. A. M. S. Gooding writes, "When I first went to Wenham the work in the converted railway carriage was well established, with Sunday School, Open Air and Gospel meeting on the Lord's Day—all fairly well attended. Every Wednesday for many years Mr. Beales ministered the Word in the garage in Capel St. Mary, mainly to the small but growing assembly, and to a number of young men whom he took over, sometimes three times a week from Ipswich. These included my cousins and others. When they began to show a measure of ability he encouraged them to preach and give simple expositions of the Word. He was an excellent teacher, a good shepherd. They were and are greatly indebted to him for his help in those formative years."

In 1934 the new Gospel Hall was opened in Great Wenham, most of the cost being borne by R. W. B.

Along came World War Two. His staff were called up for military service, and Mr. Beales was given a job with the Ministry of Defence at Cambridge. Both at Ipswich and Cambridge the War gave Reg. Beales a new sphere of service. In Ipswich a soldiers' meeting was commenced. These were for men of all three services, Ipswich being a port. There was hymn-singing, brief gospel messages and tea and cakes. The young folk of the Beales family remember joining others in "fishing" service personnel into the gospel meetings in a neutral hall near the town centre. (The story of the assemblies' outreach to service personnel has never been written, but research will show that it was extensive in many parts of the country).

No doubt this work continued in Ipswich but the Beales had to move to Cambridge in 1941. His work relating to Fire Stations took him all over the Home Counties by car. He frequently picked up service people thumbing lifts and took the opportunity of presenting them with the gospel. He had two series of gospel booklets printed, one containing the conversion stories of his friends, the other entitled "Facing Facts". He gave away hundreds of these during and after the War. (One was the testimony of John Curtis of Thunderley, who had been in training to be a R.C. priest. He was converted after he had married. Just after the War a man who had been studying in a seminary and was about to be ordained a priest read that story and was saved). Family report that night after night their dad was out visiting RAF stations around Cambridge having Bible Readings with young Christian airmen.

After the war the Beales returned to Ipswich and Reg. resumed his work as an architect, when they fellowshipped in Kemball St. Gospel Hall. Mr. Beales moved freely around the area and beyond preaching and teaching. He also began issuing pamphlets on various biblical topics like "Translation or Tribulation?",

"The Feasts of Jehovah", etc. As his oral ministry declined his written increased. He spent hours typing articles which were circulated to the people on his mailing list.

Just as he had taken a keen interest in Great Wenham between the two wars, so he took a keen interest in the Felixstowe assembly after World War Two. Numbers were small but every Lord's Day for a while he and John Stone would travel from Ipswich to help at the Breaking of Bread meeting.

Reg. Beales was so obviously an all-round servant of the Lord, using his gift and means for the Lord wherever he lived and leaving a lasting influence over family and friends. He was an old man and full of years." Andy Jelfs, Counties Evangelist in N. Essex can tell of various Christians whom he has met in the area who owed their conversion to R. W. Beales.

A. M. S. Gooding describes him as "the most gifted expositor of the scriptures in E. Anglia for many years."

ARCHIE H. BOULTON
(1884–1985)

ARCHIE H. BOULTON

Archie Boulton, or A.H.B. as he was known to many, was born into a Christian family in 1884. He was converted when he was fifteen, i.e. in 1899. From his conversion he was encouraged to witness for his Lord and it was he, who, a few weeks later, pointed his friend, Willie Clare, two years his junior, to the Saviour in a stable. He appears to have been in one of the Liverpool assemblies in earlier days, but he moved across to the Wirral, to Bebington where his life's work was done. He married his childhood sweetheart, Mary Huxley in 1909, and they had fifty years together before the Lord called her home.

Archie was a good preacher and minister of the Word and took many meetings in the Lancashire area. I found his name in bound volumes of magazines revealing that he addressed quite a number of the Scottish New Year conferences in the early thirties.

A.H.B. was a builder to trade and while he made money out of it, he used it for the Lord's glory and for people's good. He played a considerable part in the development of the town of Bebington in building projects, large and small. In particular he built hundreds of houses for ordinary people, called in those days Boulton's little palaces: It was he who introduced electricity into houses in Bebington. Building-wise he was away ahead of his time, building Bethany Crescent in Bebington for elderly people, quite a number of which were occupied by elderly missionaries in retirement like Mr. Zentler of Central Africa. Both Sir Winston Churchill and Harold MacMillan, later Lord Stockton, commended him for his services to housing. Naturally he built the hall for the local assembly in Bebington and Bethesda Hall is his monument to this day.

Mr. Boulton's missionary interest was profound. He was one of that group of Englishmen who, in the inter-war years were so involved and interested in assembly missionary work that they were regular consultants of the editors of "Echoes of Service." In his earlier days he travelled abroad widely, at a time when it was less common than now, and took a keen interest in hundreds of the Lord's servants. He often took the initiative, when economic conditions at home hurt the value of the pound to counteract this. One friend said, "It is within my knowledge that he gave thousands to missionary work and gospel work generally."

With a number of others like Prof. Rendle Short, Alec Pulleng and James Stephen he was very much involved in the Missionary Study Class movement. He played a big part in the establishment of Plas Menai, Llanfairfechan as a Christian hotel, where for many years Missionary Fellowship Weeks were held.

His later years were brightened by his second marriage to Emma Hamilton who nursed him well, and whose children and grandchildren gave him the family which he had been denied. Although he became a centenarian his mind was clear to the last and he was still talking about the future of assembly missionary work almost till the end of his life.

Dr. JOHN BOYD
(1902–1981)

Dr. JOHN BOYD

John Boyd was born into a Christian family in the Donegall Pass area of Belfast in 1902. Under the influence of Christian parents he was probably saved in childhood although he made no commitment to spiritual things until he was a doctor. The type of parents he had was illustrated in a recent obituary in "The Believers' Magazine" which said that the deceased had become aware of his soul's need in conversation with Dr. Boyd's father, Robert. The same influence is illustrated in the story that at an early age young John could recite all 176 verses of Ps. 119 by heart.

At school John Boyd's natural talents were rewarded with scholarships into Higher Education, first into the Royal Belfast Academical Institution, and then into Queen's College where he graduated in medicine in the minimum time possible. He first practised in England and it was then that he began to make open confession of his Christian faith in answer to his parents' prayers.

Returning to Ulster Dr. Boyd married Miss Lily McCleery of Crossgar, commenced to practise medicine in Ormeau Road, and sought fellowship with the Apsley Street assembly, in which he continued until 1970. Thus commenced a life of usefulness for God. On the personal level having completed his sick visits he would drive to a quiet spot on the Hillfoot Road for a quiet time in prayer and with his Book. On the domestic side their home was wide open to the Lord's servants from home and abroad. Never blessed with children they welcomed the family of the Lord's people into their home. The writer was one of those who benefitted and had to inscribe his name into the most interesting Visitors' Book he ever came across. Only while preparing this biography has it become apparent that that service of hospitality must have begun when the Boyds were just a young couple setting up house and obviously bent on using it for God from the very beginning. The first name of an eminent Bible teacher of past days recorded in that book was that of C. F. Hogg. Many others followed for Dr. Boyd became Secretary for the Belfast Christmas Conference and acted in that capacity for many years.

John Boyd didn't only organise meetings and entertain the Lord's servants; he was a Bible teacher in his own right. Brethren recall the dapper little gentleman, complete with the rosebud in his lapel, conducting some of the annual Bible Readings at Lurgan. At the other end of the scale he loved to help small country assemblies, especially Crossgar where his wife was brought up, which he visited every week until he was no longer able to drive. His written ministry was as valuable as was his oral. He contributed articles to magazines at home and abroad, particularly "Assembly Testimony", "Precious Seed", and "The Believers' Magazine". Probably his last contributions to the last-mentioned was a series on the prophetic word.

All aspects of the Lord's work were the subject of the attention of Dr. Boyd. In 1943 he added a Diploma in Anaesthetics to his qualifications and in 1948 he took his F.R.C.S. (Anaesthetics) which took him out of the hurlyburly of General Practice and gave him a little more freedom. His work for the Lord expanded into the administrative field as he joined the Council of the Retired Missionary Aid Fund in 1956, becoming its Chairman in 1966, in which capacity he continued until 1977. He was also a Director of Stewards Coy. from 1962–1978. Locally in N. Ireland he was a convener of the large Easter Conference and frequently chairman of the huge Missionary session. He was also on the Missionary Homes Committee and consultant on missionary candidates from the province. He was also one of the original committee for Faith House, the Belfast Eventide Home for elderly Christians.

The story of John and Lily Boyd wouldn't be complete without a mention of their faithful housekeeper, Molly Stewart. She was really a member of the family, attending not only to the needs of her employers but also to those of their many guests. She was the faithful companion of Mrs. Boyd after John's homecall from Hollywood where they lived and worshipped from 1970 until their homecalls.

John Boyd was an all-round Christian gentleman. A man of

prayer he had his own list of the children of missionaries for whom he prayed regularly long before a list of such appeared in the Echoes Daily Prayer Guide. At his funeral he was described as a man with "a big heart for all Christians, who did not sacrifice the principles of the Word of God which he learned by diligent study and held dear." Another described him as being happy and humble, helpful and hospitable. Such men are scarce and valuable.

JOHN BRITTON
(1911–1985)

JOHN BRITTON

"See you in the morning"

This was the usual parting of John Britton of Warrington who
was killed in a road accident on the A74 near Lesmahagow,
Scotland, on October 10, 1985 after visiting his mother at
Auchlochan House.

Born in 1911 he was born again in the Gospel Hall, Forster
Street when seven years of age, after hearing his father speak on
John 3:16. Very soon afterwards he began to distribute tracts and
then preach in the open-air, which he continued till his home-call.
At the age of fourteen he took his first Gospel meeting in Forster
Street, whilst still in short trousers, and was known as the boy
preacher.

At the church school which he attended he was always quick to
challenge the scripture teacher who insisted that nobody could be
sure of being saved, but many years later he had the joy of
knowing that his old teacher had died believing, after he had
visited him in hospital and got him to see that he could be saved
and know it.

When preparing for Gospel meetings it was his habit to learn
the whole chapter from which his text was taken, thus storing his
mind with scripture at an early age, which was still noticeable as
he preached in his last years.

Active in the large Sunday School in Forster Street many
young boys passed through his class over the years, and there are
many men in Warrington today who can remember his class, and
many in assembly fellowship who were saved through his
teaching.

When he married Irene Charnock in 1934 he could not allow

such a golden opportunity to pass without a Gospel address, so after the vows were exchanged he turned to the congregation and gave his testimony.

About this time he joined his father, Jim Britton in his furniture business, and a number of their employees over the years were led to know the Lord and are still in assembly fellowship today, and many of the Lord's servants had the use of their van for removals and even for the rescue of broken down cars.

With the coming of the war he registered as a conscientious objector and worked on the Warrington ambulances, bearing testimony to all he came in contact with in the hospital. It was at this time that he began his hospital visitation which he kept up until the end. Visiting hours were unknown to him for he just walked in, saw the sister in charge, and visited. Many sisters would send for him first, if their patients were troubled about things and wanted a helpful talk.

One of his favourite works was children's meetings, and when the assembly had the open air meeting after the Gospel meeting, with the loud speaker equipment in the van, he would hang a flannel-graph board on the back of the van and have a children's meeting.

With the coming of the lighter evenings he would hold children's meetings in the bandstand in Bank Park, Warrington which some hundreds of children attended over the years. The young brethren of the assembly used to assist with quizzes, "got its", and the stories, and so were introduced to speaking. Many went on to become regular Gospel preachers and ministers of the Word, the writer included.

With the coming of National Service many R.A.F. lads came from the camp at Padgate to Forster Street and were shown hospitality by the saints. No brother can be given hospitality unless ably supported by his wife. In this case in the Britton household the dining table would not suffice, so the door would be taken off its hinges and laid on two trestles to accommodate the company. There are still many ex-National Servicemen who will remember the new meaning of S.O.S. learned at 63 Orford Avenue table—"stretch or starve."

On moving to Almond Grove in the late fifties, he was asked by the assembly to book the missionaries for the monthly missionary meeting. Over the next ten years scores of missionaries came to the hall to speak, were entertained in the home and helped on their way, their stay being recorded on a large map in the back room, with names, addresses and a thread leading to their sphere of work. Many made return visits or stayed as they passed through Warrington as there was always a warm welcome for any of the Lord's people.

In recent years he had, on the insistence of his family, reduced his Gospel preaching to the lighter months of the year, but he was still active in the Lord's work right up to the time of his home-call.

In recent months he had added to his farewell of, "See you in the morning" another statement! "I'm not looking for the undertaker, I'm looking for the uptaker." These were his last words to Stewart Brown as he left Auchlochan House to return home, but it was not his home in Warrington at which he arrived.

The results of the labours of this true man of God, so ably supported by his wife, will only be known "in the morning". At the time of his home-call he left a widow Rene who was in intensive care at Law Hospital, Wishaw, but 17 days later she went to join her husband with the Lord.

She was a true help-meet to him in all his work and had expressed the desire that if the Lord took her husband He would also take her.

J. R. Baker

ARTHUR JAMES CHILCOTT
(1888–1983)

ARTHUR JAMES CHILCOTT

Arthur James Chilcott was born in Exeter on the 7th November, 1888. He was the eldest of a family of seven children born to James and Georgina Chilcott, who were a godly couple from Devon in happy fellowship with the assemblies of the Lord's people there. During his early years his parents moved to Lapford and then to Barnstaple. Arthur was converted as a lad of twelve, and from that time on showed a real interest in the things of the Lord. In his teenage years he had a great zeal in communicating the Gospel, and spent his spare time preaching in the Open Air and in halls throughout many of the villages of North Devon. Often he would spend the whole of the Lord's Day with one of the smaller assemblies, seeking to help them in their worship and witness.

At the time of the First World War he felt very strongly that he could not take up Military Service so registered as a Conscientious Objector. For this stand he and his family suffered considerable reproach and much misunderstanding, even from many of his brethren. It also cost him many months of imprisonment, yet his faith was strong even under this trial. He was eventually released from prison on condition that he took up work of national importance. It was at this time that he was sent to South Wales to work on the building of a new reservoir at Llwyncwtta, Llannon near Llanelli. On the first Lord's Day Mr. Chilcott, along with a brother Pearce from Birkenhead, set out on foot and walked the two miles to the nearest assembly which was at Cross Hands. Here they were warmly received and shown loving hospitality. Later Mr. Chilcott had happy fellowship with the assembly at Ammanford and was shown much kindness by brother William Herbert and family.

His gift as an evangelist was soon in evidence and it wasn't long before South Wales became his mission field. From 1918 onwards he was giving more and more of his time to the preaching of the Word, and in the summer months was almost wholly engaged in Tent Missions. On 27th June, 1919 the Swansea & District assemblies pitched a tent at Fforestfach, and Mr. Chilcott preached for fourteen weeks with some help from Capt. Elsey, of S.S. "Dongarra" from Sydney, Australia, and brother A. O. Jones of Ammanford. It is reported that large numbers were gathered in every night, with as many as 700 people on Lord's Day evenings listening to the Word faithfully spoken. On that occasion about fifty people professed to be saved, and some of them were baptised and received into the fellowship of local assemblies.

During the summers of 1920 and 1921 the tent was pitched in the Manselton and Brynhyfryd districts of Swansea and the Lord again blessed the preaching of his servant in the salvation of many precious souls. Then in 1922 the tent was erected in Treboeth, Swansea. Here again there was a great interest in the Gospel, a number were converted and encouraged in the ways of the Lord. It was following this mission that Mr. Chilcott felt exercised to establish a more permanent testimony in Treboeth; and with the help of a few other brethren arrangements were speedily made for the building of a hall for the continuation of the work. The hall was ready for occupation early in December, 1922, and from the small beginnings the work prospered under the good hand of the Lord so that in 1972, the jubilee year of the testimony, there were just over one hundred believers in the fellowship of the assembly. To this work in particular Mr. Chilcott gave himself untiringly and sacrificially.

Strange as it may seem there was combined in him the heart of evangelist and shepherd. He was truly a faithful under-shepherd to the assembly at Treboeth, for he not only cared for the sheep of His pasture but he literally carried the lambs in his bosom. He loved the little children, he was Sunday School Superintendent for many years and whenever he saw children in other meetings he always had a word for them. Often at the close of the Breaking of Bread on a Lord's Day morning he would say, Now let us sing so that the young ones can join with us in our thanksgiving,

"Jesus loves me this I know ..."

Though he gave his life to the assembly at Treboeth his zeal in the Gospel was undiminished. In 1924 the Cardiff assembles secured a tent which they called the Canvas Cathedral with seating for 2,300 people. Mr. Chilcott was invited to share in the preaching with George Ainsworth of Harrogate from 17th August to 22nd September. It was recorded that on the opening night, in spite of torrential rain, the tent was packed out and many had to be turned away. God gave power with the Word and souls were saved. During the first week, in spite of continuously stormy weather, the tent was comfortably full nightly and crowded on the Saturday night for Mr. Ainsworth's special address on, "The World's Approaching Crisis". On Lord's Day, 24th August the tent was again full long before the time of the meeting, and crowds were outside the closed gates wanting to get in. An overflow meeting was held, and hundreds of people, mainly men, heard the Gospel outside, while Mr. Chilcott spoke to the throng in the tent. Fully three thousand people listened to the Old, Old Story that night. During the second week the tent was filled nightly, the interest continuing to increase and people coming from surrounding towns and villages. It was a remarkable mission. Practically every night people were counselled and many confessed Christ. Mr. Chilcott was involved in many other missions throughout South Wales and was instrumental in leading hundreds to the Saviour, most of them going on to prove the genuineness of their profession, and many being added to the local assemblies.

On the 6th September, 1922 Mr. Chilcott married Miss Olive Holwill, the daughter of Mr. and Mrs. Henry Holwill, who were in fellowship at the George Street Gospel Hall, Swansea. Mrs. Chilcott was a true help-meet for her husband, a faithful partner, not only at home, but also in the work of the Lord. Their home was a place where many of the Lord's servants over the years were entertained and refreshed by the hospitality and fellowship extended. Though they only had one son, Gordon, they took the responsibility for the children of Mrs. Chilcott's sister, Mrs. Eleanor Anne Porter, who died at the age of 25 leaving four little ones motherless.

In the early 1920's Mr. Chilcott joined the Oil and Hardware business of his father-in-law, and proved himself to be a very successful business-man, well known in the city of Swansea and neighbouring towns for many years. However he would not let business stand in his way of serving the Lord. He continued in the work of evangelising, exhorting and encouraging the believers, and spending many hours throughout the week in sick visitation in hospitals as well as in the homes of those who were ill. This man's greatness lay, not in his wealth or social standing, but in his readiness at all times to serve others after the example of His Master. He could move among the highest as their equal, yet he would make himself at home with the poorest. One marvelled at his ability to meet the need of every situation he confronted. He could truly weep with those who wept and rejoice with those who rejoiced. He was a succourer of many.

We have referred much to his public preaching, but he was also a persistent personal worker, seeking to bring the claims of Christ to any with whom he came in contact. One incident out of many must suffice. During the visit of a Circus to the town brother Chilcott read in the evening paper that a baby had been born to one of the families and the christening was to take place in the Big Top tent. The following morning he went and purchased a white presentation copy of the Bible. He then went along to the fairground and asked to be introduced to the family with the new baby. He was directed to the caravan and on knocking was welcomed inside by the young mother. He gave her his present for the baby, explaining that in this Book she herself could find God's Way of Salvation. After telling her of the Love of God he stressed to her that it was now her responsibility to share this Good News with her child. She thanked him for his kindness and for sparing the time to visit her. As he was leaving the young mother said that no-one had ever told her that message before. Surely that Day only will reveal the results of his many labours.

Mr. Chilcott was faithful to the last, finding his greatest joy meeting with the Lord's people until just a few weeks before he was called Home on Friday, 18th November, 1983 at the great age of 95 years. He was greatly beloved by all who knew him. The large numbers who attended the funeral service at Treboeth Gospel Hall were an indication of the high esteem in which he was held, not only among the saints but also within the community.

Peter Davies

WILLIAM HENRY CLARE
(1886–1982)

WILLIAM HENRY CLARE

Willie Clare had a very long natural lifespan stretching to 96 years. His Christian life too was phenomenal lasting for 83 years. His family were not sympathetic to evangelical matters. He joked about arriving in our world just after the bonfires and fireworks displays were over, i.e. on 6th November, 1886. He was a precocious child, and eventually the family doctor advised that he should leave school and stop studying when he was 12. A friend had a chandler's business, and young Willie was happy to tour the countryside in his vehicle, serving the public.

When he was 13 he was persuaded to attend Camden Hall, Birkenhead to hear the gospel. After the meeting he had to go to the stable attached to the chandlery business to feed the horse. This done, his friend asked him to join in prayer and they kneeled on a sack thrown down on the floor. There he trusted the Saviour and entitled his testimony, "Born in a Stable" as a result. The catchy title was no doubt adopted to attract people's attention. His parents were not over-pleased and suggested that it would only be a three months' wonder. Trouble began when he wanted to be baptised and received into the fellowship of the Camden Hall assembly.

The business that he himself took up was insurance. But he was so interested in the scriptures and in the spread of the gospel that he was soon preaching, and travelling around doing this. It was his intention to become a missionary and he learned Spanish so that he could go to South America. That door not opening, he considered paying visits to Spain so that he could give missionaries a break and he himself could give ministry to Spanish Christians. Even this was prevented by family circumstances for first his mother died, and then his father, a sailor, died suddenly on his ship. Willie and his elder sister had therefore to assume responsibility for the family.

He felt that he had played his part in their upbringing and felt the Lord calling him into full-time service in 1916. That was wartime, so Willie headed for Shropshire to work among the troops in the large army camps there. He wrote special booklets for soldiers and airmen which he gave them as they were leaving for the Front. He received many letters of appreciation from the lads who were reading them in the trenches.

When the war was over Willie began a country-wide ministry preaching and teaching. He enjoyed fellowship with Thos. Holt who preached the gospel throughout Britain for around 60 years after 1865. Holt was a product of the '59 revival and enjoyed much blessing in his own preaching. Willie Clare had the joy of joining him in open air and tent work around 1925. The outcome was that he wrote a book entitled "Pioneer Preaching". He appreciated Holt's experience and methods. He also spent time in the Yorkshire Tent in the late 20's, as a photograph of him in his gospel car appears in the 75th anniversary booklet entitled "Telling Yorkshire".

Willie obviously loved open air work and sought the help of young men in this. He would persuade them to give their testimonies and so give them a start in preaching. If there were interrupters he would ask them to arrange a public debate. At one such which lasted a whole evening in the open air he announced a gospel meeting he was conducting the next evening, and at least one person accepted the invitation, attended the next evening and was saved.

Willie developed an interest in the prophetic word. He was involved in the Prophetic Witness movement. He used a large dispensational chart for his ministry. He described his chart as the longest and finest in the world." It illustrated the history and prophecy of the Bible and was twelve feet long and six deep. He entitled his talks, "World Events in the Light of the Bible". A newspaper cutting claimed that he had travelled the world preaching.

In the middle of all this Mr. Clare was again ordered to stop preaching and have a rest because he had TB. Some suggested that he should organise parties of Christians to travel abroad. He was probably one of the first to do so. The idea was that he would escort such groups of Christians personally, give them ministry daily during their holiday, meet missionaries and help to conduct services in the countries in question. In this connection he visited Norway, Sweden, France, Switzerland, N. Africa and Palestine. He had interesting sets of slides on all of them. Maybe this is how he earned his F.R.G.S.

On his physical recovery he resumed his ministry, but he had another vision. He saw the possibilities in broadcasting. Readers will know that it is not the policy of the B.B.C. to give freedom on the air. And the I.B.A. is forbidden by its constitution to allow time to be bought for gospel broadcasts. Willie Clare pestered the B.B.C. with his letters, asking for the assemblies to be given an input into their religious broadcasting programme. Eventually he was asked for details, and he visited the B.B.C. in London to discuss the matter and the privilege was granted. To begin with he was so pleased and involved that he visited whatever hall was being used for particular broadcasts and travelled the country doing so. Eventually he was invited to conduct such a broadcast himself which he did from his home assembly of Clive in Shropshire. In a nearby town to Clive pubs had radio sets placed for the hearing of the broadcast and one person trusted the Saviour. On another occasion Mr. Clare was given the opportunity of broadcasting on the B.B.C. World Service and afterwards heard from a missionary in Africa who said that he and his wife had been feeling down when they tuned in and were given a great boost. This would be the experience of quite a number of those brethren who have had this opportunity. Alas, we don't seem to be having as many chances as we had. Has Willie Clare's mantle not fallen on anybody?

William Henry Clare and Clive are inseparable. He believed that even a full-time worker should carry a sense of responsibility towards his own assembly. He claimed that this built up the assembly and trained young folk for responsibility. On one occasion he claimed to have given some 1,200 different addresses in Clive. Some time after losing his wife he married again and moved to Kilmarnock. So he spent the declining days of a very long life of service in Ayrshire. He was a remarkable man.

JIMMY CUTHBERTSON
(1903–1981)

JIMMY CUTHERBERTSON

"A lovely wee man"

Jimmy Cuthbertson was born in the mining village of Meikle Earnock, near Hamilton on 2nd November, 1903. He was the second oldest of a family of ten and that family was not Christian. When he left school at fourteen he went down the mine at which occupation he continued for 51 years. He was playing a game of football in a country lane when an old road sweeper approached him and said, "You would like to be saved. Come along with me to the Gospel Meeting on Sunday night." The following Sunday found the sixteen year-old in Low Waters Gospel Hall, Hamilton, listening to an able expositor of the scriptures, Alec Scott, father of Robert and Hugh, assisted by an up-and-coming young man, John Currie of Newmains. So on 20th June, 1920 Alec Scott pointed Jimmy Cuthbertson to the Saviour. Baptism and reception into the fellowship of the assembly followed, where he continued for the next thirteen years when he moved in connection with his employment to Halfway, Cambuslang for three years, returning to Low Waters for another fourteen years until the run-down of the Lanarkshire mining industry compelled his removal to the Lothians where the Cuthbertsons fellowshipped in Newtongrange assembly for two years, and in Musselburgh for eighteen, retiring to Hamilton and joining the Selkirk Street assembly for the remaining years of his life.

Young Jimmy was very fond of the new popular cinemas. But a new attraction had entered his life. When he quoted some of those hymns in his ministry for the rest of his life he meant every word: "There's no-one like my Saviour", and again, "That man of Calvary has won my heart from me." And he gave himself to the study of the scriptures. He formed good study habits. He regarded Saturday as a bonus in this respect, for, finished work by lunch-time, he was able to spend the remainder of the day with his Bible. And he believed that his occupation helped, for his job required enormous physical stamina, but left his mind free and fresh after he took off his pit clothes. After retirement his approach was the same. He rose early for prayer and study.

David Cook wrote about him: "He developed his own filing system, an elaborate alliterative method wholly in his mind. It served him well and enabled him to practise instant recall." The lack of education virtually demands that a considerable amount of time has to be spent on the selection of words. And this some of those old miners worked into a fine art, not only for the preacher's recall, but also for the hearers'. And so his parish extended to the whole of the United Kingdom And he never had a car so that he had many a long wearisome journey about which he never complained. Some of those journeys were unnecessarily wrong as Jimmy's geography wasn't very good so that he took the long way round sometimes. This too was done coupled with a swallowing problem which afflicted him for years. Several stretchings of his gullet gave only temporary relief, which made it impossible for Jimmy to eat normally, but he didn't make this an opportunity to restrict his service.

Jimmy Cuthbertson wasn't only a Bible teacher, warm and stirring, but he was also an evangelist, personal and public. Personal evangelism was part of his life. Originally shy he became a ready conversationalist. He loved to travel to towns and villages, large and small to preach the gospel. Time and again he got time off work to conduct gospel campaigns. One of his early ones was in the Lanarkshire village of Kirkmuirhill and there were lasting results from this. There was a bus strike during this time, so Jimmy simply cycled from Hamilton to Kirkmuirhill. Another campaign was conducted at Tranent in the Lothians and it was then that Betty Dennison, later Mrs. David Smith of Sabah and Hong Kong, was saved. A fortnight in Pendlebury, Manchester brought blessing to some. He had happy memories of a four-week campaign in Belfast. He was in Swinton, Manchester for several weeks and saw a number of women saved. He was never refused permission to stay off work to evangelise. On one occasion when he returned after a campaign the colliery manager asked, "Any conversions?" A remark made from his hospital bed near the end was; "I have had the great joy of leading many to the Lord."

Mining is naturally a dangerous occupation and Jimmy and a fellow-workman had a very narrow escape one day. They had just left their work-place when a fall of rock took place. He travelled later that same day to speak at the farewell meeting of Joyce Shackley leaving for missionary service in Borneo, later Sabah.

In days when preachers travelled by public transport wives seldom accompanied them as the cost was double. Hence Peggy's life was a lonely one but she never complained. They had over 50 years of married life and brought up two daughters.

Jimmy Cuthbertson was a humble man. He was also a happy man. He was involved in leadership and in hospitality in every assembly in which he fellowshipped. He was the kind of man whom the Lord could use, a willing servant and an appreciative listener.

His method is unforgettable. We append a few of his outlines.

AN ASSEMBLY is
    Where LORDSHIP of Christ is UNCHALLENGED
    LEADING of the Spirit is UNQUENCHED
    LIBERTY of gift is UNHINDERED
    LOYALTY to Word is UNCOMPROMISING
    LOVE to all saints is UNFADING
    LABOUR for the Lord is UNCEASING

SONG OF SONGS 2 V8–13

HOW LIBERATING—
    WINTER is Past
    WAITING is Past
    WEARINESS is Past
    WEAKNESS is Past
    WARFARE is Past

HOW LOVELY—
    FAIRNESS of Heaven
    FRESHNESS of Heaven
    FRAGRANCE of Heaven
    FRUIT of Heaven
    FELLOWSHIP of Heaven

HOW LONG?—What a MORNING
    What a MEETING
    What a MANSION
    What a MEDICINE

JOHN 14— A PEACEFUL Heart
             A PREPARED Home
             A PLEASANT Hope
             A PERPETUAL Happiness
             A PATH to Heaven

---

2 CORINTHIANS 8:8–9—LIBERALITY

The SECRET of their AMAZING Liberality

    SPONTANEOUSNESS of their ASTOUNDING Liberality

SACRIFICIAL	ACT	of their Liberality
SINCERE	AFFECTION	of their Liberality
STIRRING	APPEAL	of their Liberality
SYSTEMATIC	ARRANGEMENT	of their Liberality
STEWARDSHIP	AGREEMENT	of their Liberality
SYMPATHETIC	ATMOSPHERE	of their Liberality
SPIRITUAL	ACHIEVEMENT	of their Liberality
SWEET	ASCENDING	of their Liberality
SCRIPTURAL	ACCOUNT	of their Liberality

They QUESTIONED	His	HOLY CONCEPTION
They MOCKED	His	HUMBLE OCCUPATION
They DESPISED	His	LACK OF EDUCATION
They SPURNED	His	SPIRITUAL DEVOTION
They SPORTED	His	AWFUL CRUCIFIXION
They DENIED	His	GLORIOUS RESURRECTION

H. L. ELLISON
(1903–1983)

H. L. ELLISON

Harry Leopold Ellison was born on July 10, 1903 in Cracow in Poland, then part of Austria–Hungary. His father, Leopold Zeckhausen, was a Lithuanian Jewish grain merchant occupied with international trade. Harry's father was converted in Amsterdam through the witness of Christian colleagues and fellow-lodgers, and through the teaching of A. C. Adler, a missionary with the London Society for Promoting Christianity among the Jews, later the Church Mission to the Jews.

A few years later, Mr. Zeckhausen gave up business and trained as a missionary among his own people. He trained in London, was first sent to work in Manchester and then in 1899 to Jerusalem where he was ordained as a minister of the Church of England. (In addition to having an Anglican clergyman as his father, H. L. Ellison had a bishop on his mother's side). Here too in Jerusalem Harry's father met and later married Miss Sarah Jane Ellison, daughter and sister of Anglican ministers from Ireland, who was working as a missionary nurse in Jerusalem. They married in 1901 and were transferred to Cracow in 1902. Here both of their sons were born. Neither boy was registered as British, and were therefore officially stateless until they were old enough to be naturalised, when they took their mother's surname, at the father's suggestion. He believed that a German name might be a hindrance in post-war Britain.

As Mr. and Mrs. Zeckhausen were moved from place to place their sons had no settled home nor childhood friends. World War One resulted in the boys having to return to Ireland with their mother, while father continued with his missionary work in Rumania. Hence the boys had their secondary education in Dublin. Young Harry made some sort of commitment to the Lord when he was fourteen or fifteen, but it was not until he was at College in London that he gave his heart completely to the Lord. A missionary background made for a propensity for languages, but over confident Harry failed in his subsidiary subject of French at the end of his first degree course at King's College about 1924. Humbled he sought the Lord and developed a desire to serve Him full-time.

He attributed his Christian growth to the Crusaders, the Children's Special Service Mission and the Keswick Convention. Actually the last link in his conversion story was a man from an assembly. Anxious to serve the Lord he returned to study, this time for a B.D., at the London College of Divinity. He was then ordained as a clergyman in the Church of England and was appointed to a poor parish in South East London. He was a Tutor in the London College of Divinity from 1927–1930, but to his surprise the Lord called him to missionary work.

Receiving a clear call to work among Jews he joined the Church Mission to Jews and was sent first to Poland and then to Rumania. In the latter he met Miss Adeline Mary Todd, a Baptist with a strong Dissenting background, who was working with the Mildmay Mission to the Jews as a teacher of English in their school for Jews and Protestants. It was probably Johannes Warns' book on baptism that was the decisive factor in Harry's acceptance of the New Testament teaching on immersion, but most Rumanian Protestants are baptised, and that could have influenced. H. L. Ellison was a controversial figure and never more so when he accepted that God wanted him personally to witness to that truth. The consequent uproar resulted in the horrified bishop sacking him from his post, and, as far as he could, from the Anglican Church. It was then that he married his Baptist lady friend.

Along came World War Two and the Ellisons had to return to England. It was then that he sought fellowship with the assemblies of the Lord's people. He served the Mildmay Mission to the Jews, with whom he had been working in Rumania after his baptism, as Editorial Secretary from 1939–1949. He then lectured in various evangelical institutions like London Bible College, Moorlands Bible College, Spurgeon's College, Wiedenest Bible College in Germany, and Birmingham Bible Institute. The truth of the matter was that, liberated from the bondage of an ecclesiastical system, Mr. Ellison was not going to submit to any

40

other kind of bondage. He did refuse the offer of the Principalship of a theoretical college.

Lectureship and authorship so often go hand in hand. The most popular, as distinct from scholarly, of H. L. Ellison's books is "The Household Church". That book would alternatively please and irritate many of us. Yet, he says, "I found my home in an assembly of Christian Brethren, and I have never had reason to repent my decision". In the course of his service for the Lord he visited eleven countries and preached in over three hundred assemblies in them, as well as lecturing in eight different Colleges.

In the literary field Harry Ellison was best known for his Old Testament studies. Thus we have his book on Job entitled, "From Tragedy to Triumph". But he ventured into almost all parts of the Old Testament. The prophets are represented in "Ezekiel, the Man and His Message", the Pentateuch by "Fathers of the Covenant", eleven of which studies first appeared in "The Hebrew Christian", the quarterly organ of the Hebrew Christian Alliance. Like all of Jewish background we would expect him to give us something about the Messiah and so we have, "The Centrality of the Messianic Idea in the Old Testament," and "The Servant of Jehovah".

He was a consulting editor for both "A New Testament Commentary" and "A Bible Commentary for Today" writing the articles on Genesis, Matthew, The Theology of The Old Testament and the Religious Background of the New Testament.

Leaving London, ostensibly for retirement, Mr. Ellison fellowshipped in the assembly at Dawlish in Devon, where he passed away on his eightieth birthday.

ALBERT FALLAIZE
(1890–1987)

ALBERT FALLAIZE

"I was born in 1890 in the East End of London, not far from Dr. Barnardo's first home for needy children in Stepney Causeway. Dr. Barnardo died in September, 1905 and as a boy I often heard him preach in the famous 'Edinburgh Castle', the public house he purchased and converted into a Preaching Hall. Through his preaching and example I was converted in September, 1903 and some years later gave myself to whole-time service."

Assembly Fellowship

"In 1906 my family moved from London to a suburb, Seven Kings. An Assembly had just been formed there—South Park Chapel. I was attracted to the meetings, and there learned some of the truths we know as Assembly truth—Baptism, Breaking of Bread and Church truth. For many years Mr. Harold St. John gave a month of concentrated Bible Study at the assembly there. In the biography written by his daughter Patricia it is recorded, 'At South Park Chapel, Seven Kings he ministered annually, if in England, over a period of about 45 years .... During his ministry most of the books in the Bible received detailed attention'. The truth taught in the assembly was my Bible School. I was baptized, received into fellowship and met with the believers at the Lord's Supper, and commenced serving the Lord."

Guidance

"After nearly eight years in fellowship I was married. We both felt that we ought to give ourselves wholly to the work of the

Lord. We were Sunday School teachers, regular at all the meetings. I led the Children's midweek service. I was invited by the assemblies around to preach the Gospel, yet I did not find it easy to know the will of God for us. Personal guidance cannot be hurried. The Word of God again and again was a message for us personally. We continually prayed about it and after months of heart exercise were quietly assured it was His will to serve Him whole time. The question was, Where to serve? We were interested in God's Work in China, India and other fields, but the Muslim world was a challenge to me. Its vastness, its problems, the few who responded to the need, the few results and the difficulties encountered in preaching the Gospel. We met with the elders of the Assembly and told them of our exercise and how we felt called to service amongst Muslims. They did not seem surprised, and gave good advice—to continue in the Assembly and in the service we were engaged in, to study helpful books whilst awaiting the door to open. First as we had to learn a new language to go carefully through an English Grammar. Also as Muslims deny the deity and sacrificial death of Christ to study carefully the Scriptures about these subjects. When I came up against Muslim arguments I was thankful for their advice and help."

"In November, 1915 the way opened for us to proceed to Morocco, a Muslim country. Arabic was the language. A small number of missionaries attached to 'Faith Missions' were working in the land, but millions of Muslims had never heard the Gospel. The complete Bible was already available in Classical Arabic, but it was only understood by the educated and 90% of the population was illiterate. It was necesary to translate. It was used by the people in their homes. I worked with a committee of three to do this. The New Testament was completed and printed in 1933. It was a great help and blessing to the work, and widely used."

"Charles Gabriel (commended from Turnbridge Wells) and myself for many years travelled to the tribal markets as the tribes were subdued by the French Foreign Legion. We sold over 10,000 copies of the Scriptures to strict Muslims, and there was some precious, hand-picked fruit."

"After 32 years, in 1947, health was failing. My wife had fallen from an animal and injured her back. I was exhausted. Looking to the Lord for guidance we knew it was His will for us to return. For nine months I was in and out of hospital. It was a great experience lying in hospital wards—sometimes unable to read or pray, but only to trust. Many were praying and God answered. With faith, prayer and medical skill I was completely healed."

That was Albert Fallaize's own description of the way in which his Lord led him. Their first task on arriving in Morocco was to learn Arabic. They studied it for five hours every day and then walked around each evening trying it out on the people. Feeling they could progress more where English was not spoken they moved for six months to Tetuan and their command of the language increased.

Returning to Tangier, Albert, as the only man present, had to take complete command of the Mission—twenty five people who worked for twenty five years as houseboys or servants. It disturbed Albert that while they were likely to be believers they had never expressed their faith. Some members of the Mission were unhappy about these Arabs participating in communion. Increasingly convinced that the New Testament pattern for missionary work was equally applicable to the Arab world, he withdrew from the Mission to rely on the Lord alone, and Charles Gabriel did likewise. The two men were to travel to the tribal markets for years, selling over 10,000 copies of the scriptures to strict Muslims and seeing fruit.

In Tangier Lucy resumed her clinic for women while Albert was at hand to speak to the patients. She gathered the girls to teach them to read. This was stopped when her pregnancy resulted in her death. He had to conduct his own wife's funeral. He carried on bravely, but went down with typhoid, lying at death's door for months. The Sultan sent his personal physician, and an Arab believer looked after him. His doctor insisted that he go home to recuperate.

After five months in England in 1920 Albert returned to Morocco. A nurse from England Lucy Yarde arrived to serve the Lord. Eventually he had to visit her with an infected foot and the outcome was that they married. The Lord led them to Sallee where Lucy opened a clinic. The Lord sent supplies for nothing for twenty five years. A Christian chemist from Colchester sent drugs, etc., at cost price. Women's missionary groups sent bandages etc. Albert opened a shop to sell Bibles and this raised an outcry. Each morning Lucy saw about forty patients. Each afternoon she paid home visits, in nurse's uniform to help secure her safety, but she was threatened. Men did the shopping so Albert became acquainted with the merchants to good spiritual advantage. Both invited people to their home.

Soon a small group of Christians met in the Fallaize's home, and commenced to break bread every Sunday morning. Many disappeared and were never heard of again, so Albert felt keenly that he had to teach them the Word. He also commenced to work among the Jews, from ten–twenty meeting every Sunday afternoon. He emphasised the fulfilment of Old Testament prophecies. One day a Jewish leader arrived. The young Jews were overawed. Then he asked, "How was Jesus born? Did he say he was equal with God? How did he die?" Then he declared, "So Psalms 55:23 was fulfilled?" "Bloody and deceitful men shall not live half their days." That ended the Saturday meeting, but a few sought Mr. Fallaize privately.

Beyond Sallee, Albert's evangelisation extended to the interior villages, reached first by mule, then by bicycle, and latterly by car. Twenty miles away there was a Berber settlement in which Albert and Charles Gabriel evangelised through visiting fourteen weekly markets where they sold scriptures and preached. Suddenly their privilege was withdrawn because Europeans were stirring the tribes with communist propaganda. Permission to sell scriptures was restored, but not for preaching.

Albert's abilities as a Bible teacher were made use of with the twice annual conferences arranged from 1929 onwards at Captain Fiske's farm. As many as 120 missionaries and converts would meet on such occasions. Here too baptisms took place in the irrigation tank attached to the farm.

With the end of World War Two, Albert felt that God's call was directing elsewhere. Lucy's health was deteriorating, aggravated by a back injury incurred through falling from a donkey. They came home in 1947 and his health broke down immediately, causing him to spend nine months in and out of hospital.

Recovered, he was able to engage in Bible teaching all over Britain. For many years he gave a series of addresses in Merrion Hall, Dublin and elsewhere in Eire. He was a regular speaker at a number of the annual Bible readings throughout the U.K. like

Largs and Ayr. He joined Edwin Willy in a Gospel Tent campaign in Yeovil. But Lucy was not well and the London climate did not suit her. A lady had converted her house into five flats for nurses and they were eligible since Lucy had been a nurse. Here they lived from 1953 until Lucy was called home in 1970. Both served the Lord throughout Devon. Eventually her cancer caused Albert to restrict his movements.

On her homecall Dr. Hudson, who had commenced a Bible College in Torquay for short term training for prospective Christian workers invited Albert to join his panel of lecturers in which he figured for thirteen years. He expounded several New Testament books, and lectured on Psalms and modern cults. Eventually he shared the Hudson's home, lecturing some twenty times a year to their students and still travelling elsewhere in the Lord's service.

Shortly after Lucy's homecall Harold St. John's son, Farnham, a doctor in Morocco, invited Mr. Fallaize to engage in a teaching ministry in that land. He was eighty, and was to repeat the adventure in 1974 and 1978, accompanied by retired missionaries, Harry and Chris Ratcliffe. He took a refresher course in Arabic so that Arab believers would confide in him without the presence of an interpreter. His final visit when he was eighty eight lasted a month.

Thinking of retiring from Chelston Bible College, Albert was invited to share the home of a lady who had been converted in 1949 when he was preaching in his commending assembly, South Park Chapel. She heard him preach on, "The Man Who Went Away Sad." The next night he preached on "The Man Who Went Away Glad." That was followed by messages on, "Christ's Teaching About Hell", and then about heaven. Mary Ogden got saved to her parents' consternation. Lucy sought out her mother, made friends with her—and led her to the Lord. Mr. and Mrs. Ogden died in the early 70's and knowing of Albert's impending retirement Mary invited him to share her home. Two such worthy Christian ladies feature in this book.

So Albert Fallaize ended his days in the assembly where he began. He exercised a healing ministry after some difficulties. He continued to travel in the Lord's service. He met and spoke to the parents at the assembly's holiday club and made contacts with the headmaster of his old school. He restored his links with

Barnardo's and served the Lord in all these situations, rising to every situation in connection with Dr. Barnardo. As one of the very few who remembered Dr. Barnardo himself he was invited to participate in the T.V. programme, "Songs of Praise" when Barnardo's was featured there. He got them to put on the good Doctor's favourite hymn, "My Hope is Built on Nothing Less than Jesus' blood." This resulted in him being called on for a 45 minute programme in the series, "Home On Sunday" when to quote the compère, Richard Baker, they discussed "The many ups-and-downs in the remarkable life of a very remarkable man." A further musical programme followed containing his choice of hymns. A flood of correspondence followed, and Albert replied to each personally.

From 1983, having had an operation for cancer, and then having a pacemaker implanted, Mr. Fallaize was virtually housebound, being lovingly looked after by Mary. But his work was not finished. Neighbours and children loved to call in to see him. A young Jewess, asked why she came replied, "All the kids love Uncle and love to come and see him." He prayed with them all and they learned how real the Lord Jesus was to him. Virtually all of them came to see him after his homecall, just to look on his serene face.

So ended a remarkable life of ninety seven years. He had served his Lord in sickness and in health, from youth to old age, on the platform and in the private place, suffered much and radiated Christ through it all.

As a young man, leaving to serve the Lord in Morocco, his farewell address was based on Ephesians 5:14, "The apostle Paul, in his letter to the Ephesians, after giving some of the highest truths, speaks practically and says, 'Awake, thou that sleepest, and arise from the dead and Christ shall give thee light.' Is there anyone here who is asleep? Awake thou that sleepest! Arise, leave the world that is dead, and Christ shall give thee light! To put it in phrases we can remember, "Wake up! Light up."

At ninety five he spoke about Abraham embracing the promises of God in Hebrews 11:28. Said he, "He put his arms around the wonderful promises of God, and hugged them."

"I am in my ninety sixth year, but I am finding day by day that 'The path of the just is as the shining light that shineth more and more unto the perfect day.' (Proverbs 4:18)."

"Halleljah for the Past! We don't live in it—but we learn
from it

Halleljah for the Present! There are opportunities all around
us

Halleljah for the Future! He is coming again."

The personal part of the above in the first person was written by
Mr. Fallaize at my request for "The Believers' Magazine" in
1981. His biography, entitled "A Friend of God", written by
Roger Snook, was published by "Echoes of Service" in 1986.

JOHN FISKE
1899–1986)

JOHN FISKE

John C. H. Fiske was born of Anglican parents in Southsea, Portsmouth on June 18, 1899. His father was very devoted to the Church of England, attending every evening and twice on Sundays. Mother, on the other hand, had little time for that denomination and on her conversion separated from it completely to her husband's annoyance. Mother's influence was stronger at home, but father insisted on all five children attending church. At first the family attended a Board School. John left school at 13 and a half and served his time as a grocer. He attended evening classes at the Municipal College in this connection. Illness prevented him sitting the exams and the demands of World War One prevented him going further. John did voluntary work connected with military hospitals in the early part of the War. He tried to join up before he was eighteen without success, but he later served in the Army on the Front Line in France, and then again in Dublin during the uprising there at the end of the war.

John was religiously inclined because of his background, visiting many kinds of churches, but he was not born again until 1921. After the war he returned to his old job. He was transferred to a chain grocers, and finally got a post with McVittie & Price. He was then given his own territory in Norfolk and it was here that he first came into contact with assemblies. While John always retained a liking for the dignity of the Church of England services, he certainly appreciated assembly truths, and wrote a booklet entitled, "No Earthly Priesthood." It was in Norfolk too that John met his first wife, a widow with two children, Mrs. Francis Deal.

Returning to London the Fiskes joined the Lord's Day Observance Society. Its ideal had been appreciated by John's father who habitually polished all of the family's shoes on a

Saturday evening to avoid doing it on the Lord's Day. John was an organiser and chalked up several small victories in opposing the arranging of secular activities on Sundays. One such was the success of a Poll in Wimbledon against the Sunday opening of cinemas. Another resulted in the stopping of Sunday boxing at Bedlington. These victories were won in the early 30's.

But it was with the Scripture Gift Mission that John Fiske became well-known in assemblies throughout the British Isles from 1935 onward. First he occupied various positions in the London office of that great service agency for missionary work all over the world. He did not live to see its centenary, but he played a big part in its advancement during the second half of its first century. In particular his leadership of The Young Sowers League, as it was called in his day, and in his editorship of the magazine of that section of the Scripture Gift Mission, earned him the title by which many called him until his dying day—"Uncle John."

From London he moved to Liverpool, to the Scripture Gift Mission office there, and set up house in Southport, fellowshipping in the assembly at Bethesda Hall, eventually joining the oversight and playing a part in the setting up of two of the three "hive-off" assemblies—Woodvale and Canning Road. His final and longest-lasting job with Scripture Gift Mission was as Deputation Secretary. It has been said that John Fiske put Scripture Gift Mission on the map. He pioneered for Scripture Gift Mission in the Northern Isles, Channel Islands, Northern Ireland, and parts of Scotland. He generally stayed in the same houses on his rounds and became part of many a family. He had his own "Remembrances," setting out the names of those families for regular prayer and long after his retirement they received an annual Christmas letter from him, enclosing one of his poems or meditations.

He lost his first wife in 1971 and four years later married Mrs. Ruth Chedgzoy of Birmingham, who nursed him through several serious illnesses. His meticulousness in prayer was true of him in everything—in the care of his car which she still drives, in his public reading of the scriptures, etc. Like another of those in this collection of biographies he loved to remember the children at breaking of bread services by having something to say to them, although he never had any family of his own.

John Fiske was fond of good poetry and seems to have had a particular fondness for Hy. Baker's "Lord, Thy word abideth, And our footsteps guideth, Who its truth believeth, Light and joy receiveth," which he regularly gave out at his report meetings. His world vision is reflected in the hymn we published in the "Believers Magazine" in 1981.

AWAITING THE LIGHT

Tune: Belmont or other C. M. tune

The Lord's my shepherd and I long
That all should know Him too,
That they may have their sins forgiven
And learn His will to do.

Away in heathen lands they sit
By Satan's fetters bound,
And in death's shadow they await
The Light that we have found.

How shall they hear unless we go
His message to proclaim?
Of how He died that they might live
Through faith in His dear Name.

Then let us take this message now
That early they may see
The path of life, the way to Heaven
Where His redeemed shall be

John C. H. Fiske

C

ANDREW GRAY
(1917–1985)

ANDREW GRAY

Andrew Gray sprang from an Ayrshire famiily, from the town of Kilmarnock to be precise. His father, John, left the Baptists in Kilmarnock to seek fellowship in the old Waterloo Hall in the town. He was one of a very active group of younger men who evangelised the town and countryside. On leaving school he obtained employment with the Glasgow and South Westen Railway Company and, impressing his employers, he was promoted to a managerial post in Glasgow. Andrew sometimes spoke of being put on a train at St. Enoch Station in Glasgow as a boy to spend his holidays in Kilmarnock with grandparents.

On the death of William Inglis in 1908 John Gray took his place as a director of the famous Christian publishing firm of Pickering & Inglis Ltd. He was editor of their two monthly publications, "The Believers' Pathway" and "The Herald of Salvation". In addition he compiled a volume entitled, "Bible Helps for Busy Preachers", a popular type of publication in those days. When Henry Pickering moved to London when the firm opened up in the capital, John Gray was left in charge at the Glasgow end.

That was Andrew's background. He was educated at Glasgow High School and proceeded to Glasgow University where he took an Arts degree. On graduation he joined the large publishing house of Collins for a time before transferring to Pickering & Inglis Ltd., his father's company until his homecall in 1985.

When World War Two came along Andrew joined the Navy. He rose to the rank of Lieutenant and for some act of bravery about which he never spoke he was awarded the D.S.C. This was so characteristic of the man. Andrew married Lois Sinclair from the Glanton brethren. Her sister, Jean married T. B. Rees, the well-known evangelist, and was co-host of Hildenborough Hall

Christian Conference Centre with her husband.

Andrew Gray's entire Christian life was spent in Albert Hall, Glasgow. He put this fellowship first in his thinking and would only rarely put other calls for help before it. Naturally he became a leader, and when the assembly commenced an outreach in the South Nitshill district of the city the Grays were very much involved.

But Andrew's outlook was larger still. In 1953 he became one of the Treasurers of the Home and Foreign Missionary Fund, the Missionary Service Agency that gives guidance to prospective missionaries from Scottish assemblies, and forwards gifts to them wherever they are on the world mission field. He built up a considerable knowledge of missionary matters, and he and his wife visited missionaries in several countries although he didn't take kindly to hot climates. Andrew also became a director of the Scottish Stewards Company, the Holding Company to which the property of Scottish assemblies can be transferred Not only did he become a director of the similar United Kingdom Stewards Trust, Ltd., but he became Chairman of that organisation.

Many other responsibilities were loaded on to the shoulders of this willing servant of the Lord, like Treasurership of the Widows' and Orphan's Fund which provides financial support to the widows and orphans of U.K. missionaries from assemblies. He was a founder-member of the assembly-based Scottish Counties Evangelistic Movement. He was involved in the Aitchison Trust, administering a bequest which is now almost a century old, and gives practical support for the furtherance of the gospel both at home and abroad. He was on the Council of the Retired Missionary Aid Fund, all of which required considerable amount of time and effort, most of which is not understood by the majority of assembly Christians.

Andrew followed his father as one of the conveners of the now defunct Glasgow Half Yearly meetings, which made excellent ministry available to Scottish Christians for more than a century. He succeeded his colleague, Cecil Pickering as assemblies link-man with Register House in Edinburgh for licensing brethren to officiate at weddings in a system not known elsewhere in the British Isles.

Andrew Gray was also involved in the work of quite a number of missionary support groups. For instance, he was the assemblies' representative on the National Bible Society of Scotland, chairman of the Gospel Radio Fellowship, member of the Scripture Union Council, etc. All of this was done with quiet efficiency for Andrew Gray said little about his extensive contribution to the Lord's work. And the Grays still had time for visitation. He was just past retirement age when the amalgamation of Pickering & Inglis Ltd. with Marshall, Morgan and Scott took place, and this gave him the opportunity to retire. He was looking forward to a well-earned retirement when he went down with a serious illness. The outcome was that the Lord took him home at the comparatively early age of sixty eight. Assemblies owe a great deal to such.

GEORGE HARPUR
(1910–1987)

GEORGE HARPUR

George Harpur was a native of Dublin city in the South of Ireland. His upbringing was in the Church of Ireland where he was both christened and confirmed. Throughout childhood and youth he attended Sunday School and Bible Class there, and fully participated in the young people's activities. From the age of six he showed a fondness for books which continued with him for the rest of his life.

George also attended the Boys' branch of the Dublin Y.M.C.A. which was then led by the famous Captain Reginald Wallis, author of "The New Life" series of books for young Christians, possibly the first such series produced by Christian publishers. When he was seventeen George Harpur, one of a group of five young men, trusted the Saviour. They all went on for the Lord, held occasional reunions, and went on to become faithful servants of the Lord.

It was the intention that George would become a Civil Servant but instead he became a commercial traveller, which occupation proved to be a good preparation for his life's work. First his business contacts broke down his natural reserve, while overnights in hotels were spent in Bible study. The weekends at home were occuped with preaching.

But George Harpur soon felt called to full-time service for the Lord. Stepping out in faith he crossed to London to the Honor Oak Christian Fellowship, with which he spent two and a half years learning how to do pastoral work and engaging in Bible teaching and evangelism in Missions and Chapels. Towards the end of that time he came into fellowship with assemblies of the Lord's people with which he continued until the Lord took him home.

In those pre-war days George Harpur was an evangelist. He

worked a lot with Luther Rees and engaged in gospel campaigns, both indoors and in tents with others like John McAlpine and Harold Wildish.

It was during this period that he married Ruth Jeffers of Bandon in Ireland, whom he had met on his rounds in his commercial traveller days and fell in love with her at first sight. However marriage was not possible until 1935 and this required the setting up of a home—in Bournemouth.

Along came World War Two which upset the peacetime routine of almost everybody including the Lord's servants. George Harpur combined his preaching with administrative work connected with the Air Raid Precautions Service—the old name for Civil Defence—based at Muller's Homes in Bristol. He seized the opportunity to arrange Sunday services for A.R.P. staff at which attendances of a thousand were not uncommon. Here their only son was born.

Assembly Christians had long been noted for their Bible knowledge. The war years made George Harpur realise that that was no longer true. He decided on a change of direction in his Christian service to give more of his attention to Bible teaching. This was to be his passion for the remainder of his life and took him into corners of the United Kingdom where he had not been before. He came to the old Glasgow Half Yearly Meetings, he partnered brethren like Harold St. John and E. W. Rogers at the Ayr, Largs and Aberdeen Bible Readings, but above all he conducted the annual Glasgow Summer Bible School from 1956 until 1986. This met on Monday and Friday evenings for a whole month, and attracted young Christians from a wide area to Anniesland Hall in the West End of the city. After an initial introduction those attending would choose which group they wished to join from the following: The Biblical Exposition Group, the Outreach Group, the Devotional and Practical Group and the Introductory Group. Each student attempted to answer the questions on the appropriate Study Sheet and then joined his group to compare notes. This continued for thirty years, during which time his beloved wife was called home, while the 1987 one was planned, but the Lord's servant was called home a few months beforehand. An off-shoot Bible School also ran in Ayr for a few years.

George Harpur was very much at home at residential

conferences, especially for young people, and his help was greatly appreciated at the biennial conferences of the Counties Evangelistic Work for their evangelists.

On the personal level the Harpurs moved from Bristol in 1956 and joined the Brentwood assembly in Essex where they continued until the Lord called them home. George had just remarried when his end came. As indicated he died in full harness.

Writing for "The Harvester" just shortly before his end, one of the brethren from Brentwood said, "George stands out as a man with a wide vision, yet who still believes in 'assembly principles'; as a man of deep Biblical knowledge, yet who is approachable with the simplest question; as a man who carries out a daunting timetable, yet who has always time to advise and help."

One of the biggest problems in a busy life is to get time to write. It is therefore not surprising that the only book that came from George Harpur's pen was a comparatively small one entitled, "Meet the Book", which was published in 1970. Mabye that's the kind of book which we should have come to expect from a man who was as interested in Bible schools.

JEFFREY HARRISON
(1909–1990)

JEFFREY HARRISON

Jeffrey Harrison was born into a religious home. In the service of religion he learned the organ and before the age of seventeen was deputy church organist, although in heart and often in life he was a rebel. His first job was as a film projectionist, but later he worked on the railway. It was there he met George Barton. George invited him to his wedding at the old wooden Gospel Hall in Widnes. Returning from the honeymoon, George and his wife invited him to Sunday tea and then to the gospel meeting. It was the first time he had heard the gospel, but as he said later, he had been under deep conviction for two years. He was converted that very night. He was surprised to find that his family were far from pleased at his decision, especially when he was baptised and received into fellowship at the Gospel Hall at the age of nineteen.

He was soon afterwards made redundant but used his time to study the Word of God. He would stay up studying until two o'clock in the morning despite opposition from the family who allowed him only a candle to study by, complaining that gas was too expensive. However his faith was rewarded and eventually he saw his mother, grandmother and brother saved, baptised and received into fellowship in Widnes.

This early experience gave him a conviction about assembly truth that he never lost. He took his first gospel meeting twelve months after he was saved. It was in Manchester and he had the joy of seeing a woman converted. He began to take ministry meetings as well, and by the 1930's he had become committed most evenings and weekends. He married his wife Hilda in 1939, a marriage God blessed with seven daughters.

Mr. Harrison was a conscientious objector in the war and eventually obtained employment as a caretaker in Bromborough. He held this position until 1949, by which time he was so busy that he was considering becoming a full-time worker. He was invited to take a series of meetings in Kent beginning on the first of September. He had prayed for the Lord's guidance about any decision. He had been told that he was to be made redundant six weeks before that date, but this was later changed to the last day of August. Thus he ended work on the Friday and took up full-time service on the Saturday! By this time he had become well known in many parts of the country and his long association with South Wales had begun.

In 1951 he was invited to take over the Counties Evangelistic work in Norfolk, which he did, and commuted for two years until the family moved with him to Norwich. This summer work centred on tent and caravan. He specialised in evangelising villages with no testimony and after long and patient work saw two or three assemblies established. He also began the Norfolk camp work for boys and girls. During the winter he ministered throughout the country.

In 1960 the family returned to Merseyside and Mr. Harrison's ministry widened, not only in England and Wales, but eventually in Scotland, Northern Ireland, Belgium, Holland, Malaysia and South Africa (which he visited twice).

His favourite ministry was the often neglected Old Testament. He also had a wonderful strategic grasp of God's purpose through the ages. He used a number of charts to good effect. His "Seven World Crises" chart involved a combination of Bible history and prophecy together with the gospel. His characteristic style was unforgettable and he abhorred notes! He ministered until his 79th year, thus fulfilling forty years in full-time service.

He had a long and painful illness for the last eighteen months of his life which was patiently borne.

The assembly truths he taught so clearly were paid for dearly in his early life. The gospel message he heard and immediately believed became immediately something to tell others whatever the cost. He often said that God had never let him down and he had never asked for a meeting. He was a serious man doing serious business for God.

J. R. Baker

STUART HINE
(1899–1989)

ALEC McGREGOR
(1898–1989)

STUART HINE

ALEC McGREGOR

Both missionary brethren had so much in common that a combined story seems appropriate. Both were born within a year of each other, although in different parts of the U.K. Both served the Lord in Eastern Europe—in Poland, Russia and Czechoslovakia. Both were expelled from Eastern Europe by political forces, but continued to serve the Lord in the homelands among people who came from the lands from which they were expelled, and both were involved in relief work for the people of the lands where they had formerly served the Lord. Finally both were called home to glory in the same year, although again a few hundred miles apart in the U.K. Alistair McGregor felt that his experiences in early life were very similar to those of Sonia Hine.

Outwardly Stuart Hine's chief claim to fame would be as the translator/author of "How Great Thou Art", but that was the product of several incidents in a life of faithful service for the Lord Jesus. He was born into a Salvation Army family in Hammersmith and dedicated as a child in the Citadel. His conversion took place at Gospel meetings conducted by the converted actress, Madame Annie Ryan. As a 14-year-old Stuart trusted the Saviour in a theatre or music hall after she sang, "It is not try but trust, Tis His great work that saves us, It is not try but trust." Two months later he submitted to what the Salvation Army does not—believers' baptism. Baptisms for the new converts took place on successive nights as there were so many, and Stuart's turn came up on the Thursday along with 20 others.

Immediately the lad took his stand for the Lord. At school in Stepney he read his Bible at breaks and was surrounded by boys shouting, "Hine's turned religious." His first job was with the Egypt & Levant Steamship Company, as a clerk until he was called up in 1917. On his first night in barracks he again nailed his colours to the mast by getting down on his knees to pray. Like other young soldiers in this situation he was pelted with bottles, boots, lumps of coal, etc. His example prompted another young Christian to introduce himself and promise that he would acknowledge God in this way for the remainder of his army service. They met each other later in France and the young fellow thanked Stuart for making him give the promise that changed his life.

Meantime Alec McGregor's life was pursuing a similar course. He was brought up in an assembly home in the little town of Renfrew in Scotland. His time came for being called up and he registered as a Conscientious Objector, joining the same Company of the N.C.C. as W. F. Naismith, P. J. Horne, etc., with all the fellowship and training experienced in that group of young Christians.

Stuart's conscience was stirred when a Christian stepped into the ranks of his Company when marching to the troopship at Dover, holding out a promise box. Stuart's promise was: "The Lord shall fight for you, and you shall hold your peace." (Exodous 14:14). His regiment replaced one of which only 36 men survived. In the trenches Stuart pointed a young fellow to the Saviour but he was one of the many who perished while young Hine escaped with a leg wound.

Back in Civvy Street, Stuart resumed preaching the gospel. The streets of London were his pulpit and Training College. His father had turned to Socialism and their home was frequented by Labour Party Leaders whose open air meeting techniques were borrowed by young Stuart.

While Alec McGregor was brought up on assembly truths, Stuart learned them one by one. He worshipped at Manor Park Baptist Chapel, whose pastor, P. J. Smart was a protegé of Spurgeon. Both owed much to Spurgeon who had written, "As oft as you eat this bread"—once a month is not very often. Coming to the Lord's table every Lord's Day for twenty years I have enjoyed the closest of fellowship with my Lord." Thus the young man learned a second New Testament practice before he even knew about assemblies.

A third lesson was learned, also from Pastor Smith, who would say every Lord's morning: "Will some brother lead us in thanksgiving for the bread?" A sister once did so, so Pastor Smith repeated tersely: "Will a brother now lead us in giving thanks for the bread?"

It was in 1921 that Stuart Hine and his fiancée became interested in Eastern Europe. Mr. and Mrs. David Griffiths were working among Russian refugees in Poland with the Russian Missionary Society. He came home to report on his work, and Miss Salmon declared her own interest. When Stuart proposed marriage she told him that she had volunteered to serve God in Eastern Europe. A night in prayer convinced him that with or without her, Eastern Europe was God's chosen sphere of service for him. They attended the Society's prayer meetings, but nothing seemed to be happening about them, when suddenly he was told that he was required for Berlin immediately. So 1923 found him in Berlin serving in all-day-long tea meetings for some of Berlin's four million refugees. His fiancée was employed in the Society's London office and felt restricted. Both resigned from the Society and stepped out "in simple dependence on the Lord for both guidance and support."

They married in 1923, a gift enabling them to have a brief honeymoon. They arrived back in London without a penny. His mother was questioning the wisdom of returning to Europe without the backing of a Missionary Society, when an anonymous gift of £100 arrived and they went to Poland in July. They felt that the Lord was calling them to work among Russians. They obtained accommodation in Zaolbunovo, 15 miles from the Soviet border. The assembly there was the result of Bible teaching by G. H. Lang and consisted of Ukrainians, Russians, Poles, Germans and Jews. Along with E. H. Broadbent they visited the district by sleigh.

The Hines' needs were met in remarkable ways. Their need of furniture was met by her brother sending money from South Africa. They lived for six weeks on a sack of haricot beans. The Griffiths followed their moves with interest and decided to follow their example by leaving the Society and embarking on a life of faith. So in 1924 they joined the Hines who accompanied Stuart to Radzivillov and felt that God wanted them to work there. A disused brewery became the Gospel Hall and was packed every evening. When the believers broke bread a large crowd of unsaved always stood watching.

In 1927 Alec and Jean McGregor got married and, commended by the Renfrew assembly, arrived in Poland. They settled in Mlynov, the centre of the area. Miss. Rees from Wales joined them in 1928 and later married a native brother, Mr. Shneidrook. The district became the most evangelised district of Poland. "That sphere of service was so fruitful," wrote Alec McGregor, "that soon along the Russian border a good number of assemblies was formed, and going on for the Lord." (Written in 1987).

Before 1930 Bibles were very scarce. Individual Christians would learn whole books by heart, and when required to recite them by the preacher were able to do so. Letters from believers on the Soviet side of the border were censored so relatives used a Bible-based code to communicate with each other. This annoyed the secret police so that on one occasion a group, including the Hines, on their way to the weekly Bible study, were arrested and locked up overnight.

It was in 1932 that the Hines felt compelled to move to Czechoslovakia because of attempts from Warsaw to centralise assemblies. Foreign workers were finding that their residential permits were being cancelled. Stuart had visited Ruthenia in Czechoslovakia in 1928 and had written to his wife in England: "If ever the door closes in Poland I have found a land where half a million Russian people are just waiting for the gospel." There were only half a dozen evangelical companies in Ruthenia, but sixty two companies of Jehovah Witnesses. Czechoslovakian exiles in America brought this cult with them when they were able to return to their own country when it obtained independence in 1919.

Mr. Hine joined Alfred Maltzman in editing a magazine called "Grace and Peace" in 1929. Its circulation doubled when it was introduced to Ruthenia. Its early contents included the early chapters of Broadbent's "The Pilgrim Church" in Russian. This and series by Stuart on the deity of Christ and the Second Coming caused fifty five of those companies of Jehovah Witnesses to change their ground.

As in Russia Bibles were scarce. Retreating from Ruthenia in 1915 a Russian soldier dropped his Bible, and it was found by a woman in Solotchin. It lay unread until 1934 when she learned to read. Slowly she spelt out John 3:16 publicly and half a dozen were truly converted. Stuart Hine arrived in time to hear the story, which prompted the writing of the third verse of "How Great Thou Art". "And when I think that God, His Son not sparing, Sent Him to die, I scarce can take it in, That on the cross my burden gladly bearing, He bled and died to take away my sin."

In 1937 the McGregors too moved to Czechoslovakia, the Polish Government having decreed that missionaries must leave the country. Here again all three couples travelled widely in the cause of the gospel. Travel was by bicycle and the McGregors reached Czechoslovakians, Hungarians and Russians and saw much blessing in remote villages. This work continued until the war clouds gathered over Central Europe because of Adolf Hitler's ambitions.

Stuart Hine's first work in the U.K. was among evacuees, whom he found to be as ignorant of the gospel as any Hottentot. In Poland and Czechoslovakia he had done translation work for the Foreign Office and used the diplomatic bag to get Scripture Gift Mission portions translated, printed, and sent back to those countries. He continued to work for several Government Departments during the Second World War.

If the Lord's servants were no longer able to serve among East Europeans in their homelands, they now found that many people from those lands were located in Britain—Free Czechs, Free Poles, etc. Ransome Cooper, whose story is contained in "They Finished Their Course"—first series, took the lead in meeting the needs of these refugees. Thus began "The Gospel to Britain's Guests". These were offered free Christian literature through advertisements in the newspapers begun to meet their needs. Fred Butcher worded the Czech advert, while Stuart Hine did so for the Polish one. Alec McGregor sought out Polish troops stationed around Britain and learned their language for the sake of reaching them with the Gospel. The Polish Gospel Booklet Scheme offered free New Testaments. While Alec travelled the East coast conducting services for these, Jean attended to the postal requests from their home in Ayrshire. Many were saved.

Stuart Hines had been hospitalised for over a year with a compound fracture of the femur when he received a telegram from Ransome Cooper advising him that 2,000 Russian soldiers were quartered in empty hotels in Worthing. He travelled in a wheel chair in the guard's van of a train and addressed three meetings that weekend attended by 75, 100 and 150 Russians respectively. Each received a copy of the paragraphed New Testament. He led one man to Christ.

At the London Missionary Prayer Meeting in 1943 Stuart called for preparations to be made for relief work when missionaries might be able to return to their former spheres of service. In all some £80,000 was distributed in such lands through missionary brethren. Refugees flooded into Britain and each received a welcoming letter in their own language offering free New Testaments. Brethren Hine, Griffiths, Shneidrook and McGregor joined forces for this work and visited hundreds of camps to reach such people. The reception centre was at Havant which was visited every weekend by Mr. Hine. They were invited into the Hall by loudspeaker, each group in their own language. The Word was preached in three languages, depending on which group was most represented at any time. Some were saved and baptised.

This work inspired another verse of "How Great Thou Art!" Many refugees longed to be home so Stuart wrote: "When Christ shall come, With shout of acclamation, To take me home, What joy will fill my heart." As Stuart remarked: "A place for the displaced, a Home for the Homeless, a blessed Hope for the Hopeless."

The Earl's Court assembly made their hall available for these services, conducted by brethren Hine and Griffiths. The first week eight attended, the next eleven, the third sixteen and one professed conversion. And so attendances increased. Hymnbooks in Polish, Ukrainian, Russian, Czechoslovak, Yugoslav and Hungarian were used.

Postwar years saw the Lord's servants pursue refugees and emigrants seeking them for Christ. The Inasmuch Relief Fund supplied them with material benefits for these unfortunates. Messrs. McGregor and Griffiths proceeded to Norway, Sweden and Denmark, then on to Hamburg where many Slavs were being taken care of. On to Villach on the Austrian–Yugoslav border, then to Liege to contact Polish miners. Alec made another visit to Poland and Finland, Germany and Austria with time again spent among Slav groups in France and Belgium. Visits were made regularly to small groups of Polish Christians formed in this country.

With advancing age such visits became too arduous but service continued. Correspondence, literature, radio programmes, material help for new halls, etc.... And so it went on until he was suddenly called home from Auchlochan House early in 1989, the same year in which his colleague, Stuart Hine was called home from his home in Frinton. It was almost that they "had been lovely and pleasant in their lives, and in death they had not been divided."

Alistair McGregor summed up his parents' lifework like this, "Time and again doors closed for my father and mother. After nine years of blessing in Eastern Poland, years of happy fellowship with the Hines, Griffiths and Shneidrooks in service that saw a remarkable outpouring of blessing that bears fruit until this day in the vigorous assemblies of Western Russia, the Polish Government decided that all missionaries should leave. The end of service? Not at all. The Lord led to work among the same kind of people in the eastern tip of Czechoslovakia. The devastation of war came with a forced return to Britain. The end of service? No. Within months the Polish army arrived in Britain and the war years were spent in constant work among these troops. In 1945 the war ended, the Poles returned to their land, while Eastern Europe was shut off by an impenetrable Iron Curtain. The end of service? No. Over Western Europe were camps of displaced persons from Eastern Europe. Endless trips followed, sharing relief, teaching the Word, often staying in camps in conditions of real privation. Gradually the displaced persons dispersed to many parts of the world, not a few rejoicing in the Lord. End of service? No. The Iron Curtain gradually opened and teaching trips to Poland, Czechoslovakia, Yugoslavia and finally Russia itself took place.

"In every aspect of his stewardship Alec had a hidden but striking faithfulness. His prayer life was regular and extensive. Notebook after notebook was filled with careful notes of teaching prepared in Russian and English. The money entrusted to him was meticulously accounted for. Little was ever spent on himself."

Jean followed him into the Lord's presence equally quietly and suddenly just a few months later than Alec.

Stuart Hine's autobiography was issued in three parts over a number of years. It was then issued in combined form. The titles of all three parts was, "Not you, but God."

HOWARD HITCHCOCK
(1901–1983)

HOWARD HITCHCOCK

It is sad to remember Howard C. Hitchcock in the first year when the famous Westminster Missionary Meetings in which he played such a big part will not be held. He was a convener from 1949 and chaired many of the gatherings. It could be said that he had two spiritual interests—Brook Street Chapel, London and missionary work, especially in France.

Howard was born in 1901 into a Christian home. He never forgot hearing Will Payne of Bolivia at a large missionary meeting when he was just five describe how he had been saved from being burned alive. He nearly died with appendicitis when he was ten. Special prayer was made for him at Brook Street Chapel, Tottenham and he did not only recover, he got saved.

When he was twelve Howard got an invitation from a man outside his school to attend a schoolboy's Bible Class on Friday evenings at Stamford Hill where he profited from the Bible teaching of men like the Goodman brothers, etc. The leader of this class devoted his summers to Gospel work and in 1913 young Howard camped with him for a fortnight while preaching from a tent and caravan in Sussex villages. This continued until 1929, almost all of his free time being spent with tent and caravan in Sussex villages.

He had been baptised at Brook Street Chapel with seven others in 1915. He left school at about the same time, having the desire to become a chemist, inspired by his reading of the Children's Encyclopaedia. His method of qualifying had to be through evening classes four nights per week. While the chief reason for becoming a chemist this way was financial, his father's business having failed because of the war, he found it worked to his advantage, because those returning from the forces to embark on university careers, found jobs difficult to come by in the early

20's, while Howard was well established with the firm of Burt, Boulton & Haywood by that time. He served that company until he retired.

Elsie Phillips joined the Brook Street fellowship in 1921, and while Howard admired her reason—a desire for the better Bible teaching she could get there, her singing ability and her godliness, he was anxious to find out if God wanted him to be a missionary before he committed himself to a young lady.

From 1922 Howard was receiving invitations to help in open air work and gospel meetings. When his studies were completed he was able to give more time to Bible study and teaching. An unexpected gift of £25 thrust him into the business of supporting missionary work. F. W. Pucknell, newly gone to China, was the recipient of part of that, and so began a lifelong friendship, resulting in the Pucknells sharing their home on furloughs and Mrs. Pucknell during a lengthy illness. There were no Missionary Homes in those days.

Howard's company had interests in Belgium and all of his visits to countries abroad in connection with their business, gave him opportunities to visit Gospel Halls and have fellowship with missionaries. He became specially interested in France, and became very familiar with missionary work in that land so that "Echoes of Service" made use of his knowledge.

Nor did his interest in the homeland diminish and he could report conversions, both in local preaching, and in tent work with Evangelist J. K. Gemmell in Sussex in which he engaged until 1929, and of people who went on to become missionaries or capable Christian leaders. In 1927 he took over the Bible Class at Brook Street.

It was 1931 before he married Elsie and that year they were able to have their holiday in France. He had previously met a French evangelist, Rene Zinder, and a lifelong acquaintance was maintained with an interest in the Vichy district. Knowing that business and the Lord's work were going to take him to that country he learned the language.

Needing another house the Hitchcocks wanted to remain in the same assembly. They certainly believed in divine guidance in everything, and they got their new house that way too. They got the house in 1932 and the next year they were asked to accommodate Mr. and Mrs. Bryant of the Argentine at

Westminster Missionary Meeting time and that was the beginning of years of hospitality to missionaries. The following New Year's Day they had fifty four believers to a meal followed by a further talk by Mr. Bryant about his work.

World War Two brought damage and destruction both to Brook Street and to his works by air raids, and it was two years before the Chapel was repaired. Some fifty of their young folk were in the services and assembly activity plus contacts with France were severely restricted. It was 1946 before he could revisit France. It was to Brittany he went because he had a keen interest in the children's home there set up by Mr. and Mrs. Johnson to whom he took suitcases of relief, and from there he had to proceed to Vichy to see how his friends there were faring. Next item of service was the prolonged nursing of Mrs. Pucknell.

The War greatly slowed down the going of new missionaries to the world fields. A missionary candidates class was begun in Mr. Moscrop's office in the West End and this was attended by twenty–twenty five young people heading for the mission field, including Geoffry Bull. The Bible teaching was given by J. B. Watson and E. W. Rogers.

Having had to do without a car during the war, Howard was reluctant to become dependent on it in time of peace. After all walking and using public transport gives far greater opportunities for contacting people. The car, however, took them to France that year where he helped in a Whit Monday conference. For the following twenty five years they travelled to France and rejoiced in the expansion of the Lord's work. Visits of a business nature to Belgium gave him the opportunity to visit assemblies in Brussels and Charleroi and to make the acquaintance of the Polish assemblies in those parts. He would cross on Saturday afternoons, call at the hotel chosen by his company, and walk to the assembly on Sunday morning and receive the opportunity to speak.

Unfortunately Brook Street never flourished after the war as it did before it, but Mr. Hitchcock's involvement with the annual Westminster Missionary Meetings was increasing. And his missionary interest was expanding. Business trips to America enabled him to have fellowship with the C.M.M.L. brethren there.

Business-wise Howard had become a director. He decided that

he would retire at sixty five. At his farewell dinner he told the staff that he had not done any of the things that were usually supposed to enable one to get promotion. Just as chemists were obliged to test every experiment they have made, so in the school of life he had tested and approved the teaching of the scriptures under which he had been brought up.

He continued going to Belgium for his company as nobody else spoke French. 1969, '70 and '71 were busy for the Lord in France and England. After two visits to France and participation in a Bible Exhibition in Tottenham he took a stroke from which he did not fully recover. He decided that it was time to leave the London Missionary Meetings to younger men and retired in 1980. They were spared to celebrate their golden wedding in 1981, but Howard Hitchcock was nearing the end of his pilgrim journey. He was called home on July 30, 1983.

G. C. D. HOWLEY

Cecil Howley came from Southern Irish stock. As might be expected that meant that his family was Roman Catholic. His father was a theatrical producer, a profession not noted for its affluence. Young Cecil came to London while still in his teens and somehow found himself in contact with an assembly of Christians. No matter how young he was he immediately showed a deep interest in divine things.

It was almost a matter of lifting himself up with his boot-laces. Not only was he self-taught but he also managed to get enough Greek and Hebrew to be a careful expositor of the scriptures. The result was that while he was still in his early twenties he was an acceptable minister of the Word among assemblies in South-East England. His name appeared on conference cards as early as 1932 when he would just be twenty four years of age.

It has long been a feature of assembly life that evangelists welcomed keen young Christians to assist them in holiday time. That way evangelists could have the fellowship of younger men, and younger men could serve an apprenticeship in that kind of work. It is on record that young Howley assisted the Bentall brothers in Cornwall, one of the most difficult of English counties gospel-wise, during his holidays.

It is a good guide as to the value of a man's gift in Bible teaching if the demands made on him make it difficult for him to continue with normal employment. The result was that from the early forties Mr. Howley was well-known in many parts of the British Isles for his Bible ministry. He was one of the generation who loved to read from the Revised version of 1881, and in Ulster in particular young men hurried to obtain a copy for themselves after they had heard him.

For quite a number of years W. W. Fereday and Harold St.

John conducted several of the annual Bible Readings in Scotland in particular. Once Mr. Fereday dropped out for reasons of ill-health, it was Cecil Howley who joined Mr. St. John in that partnership. He was one of the younger men whom Harold St. John encouraged in his later years to help with continuity of ministry after he had gone. Cecil acquired a great respect and fondness for the elder statesman, and gathered a large collection of his letters and notes which were bequeathed to the Christian Brethren archive in the John Rylands Library of the University of Manchester after he had been called home. Indeed Mr. Howley was one of Mr. St. John's last visitors and spoke at his funeral service.

That didn't mean that the two men always agreed. There has always been disagreement about who constitute the "house of God, the church of the living God" in Tim. 3:15. It was Mr. Howley's turn to introduce the subject and he indicated that he and Mr. St. John differed on the definition. While Mr. St. John took the idealistic definiton of a New Testament church, Mr. Howley took the realistic. The writer has never felt the need of a better explanation.

That partnership ended when Mr. Howley went off on the first of two round-the-world tours of assemblies in North America and the Antipodes. He had become Assistant Editor of "The Witness," the best known of assembly magazines in its day. He was assisting J. B. Watson, its third editor and preparing to take over from Mr. Watson. Meantime his contributions appeared over the pseudonym, Touchstone.

Increasingly Cecil Howley's work was "The Witness". He did make a second world tour and that required the enormous task of preparing copy in advance for the twelve monthly issues that would appear in his absence. His oral ministry from then on was largely in the Home Counties area. His later years were bedevilled with illness, which the amputation of a leg didn't cure. Latterly John Polkinghorne took over as editor with Cecil remaining as Consultant Editor. After that long and painful illness he was called home at the age of seventy two.

Mr. Howley didn't leave any books of his own writing. His predecessor on "The Witness" edited two symposia, one on "The Faith" and the other on "The Church". Howley's contribution was, "The Church and the Churches". But his major work in the field of written ministry was the editing of "The New Testament Commentary", which Pickering and Inglis Ltd. looked on as their major publication. Assembly writers were called on to produce articles on each New Testament book while Mr. Howley was assisted in the editing by Harry Ellison and Prof. F. F. Bruce. This was followed by its Old Testament equivalent entitled "A Bible Commentary for Today", although not all contributors to it were assembly men. The latter was completed just the year before Cecil was called home. It is interesting to note that this volume is being re-issued which shows how successful it was considered.

When J. D. Douglas, a Church of Scotland clergyman was compiling "The New International Dictionary of the Christian Church", published by Zondervan and the Paternoster Press it was to Cecil Howley that he went for the articles on the Plymouth Brethren and John Nelson Darby, regarding him as an eminent leader among assemblies.

For most of his life Mr. Howley was associated with Montpellier Hall in Purley, Surrey.

ERIC HUTCHINGS

Eric Hutchings was a Mancunian who became known throughout the English-speaking world as the leader of city-wide crusades and as a radio evangelist. Professionally he was a lawyer employed by a large Insurance Company; spiritually he was a member of the Didsbury assembly from his early years. At the age of sixteen he was already known as "the boy preacher".

He became well known in evangelical circles in the city for his evangelistic work among the men of the armed forces. As a result the Forces Christian Fellowship was founded, hundreds being brought to their free teas in their premises in Wood Street. He was also one of the leaders of the North Manchester Evangelistic Campaign. Stuart Hine, unable to operate on the continent of Europe during the war years, described a visit he paid to that city in connection with his work among European troops based in England. He found that a cinema had been taken for gospel meetings and a banner erected declaring, "All Next Week: 'It Started With Eve'. Come to the N.M. Evangelistic Campaign and see what started with Eve." Stuart Hine also remarked that there were many Free French servicemen there and Eric Hutchings made sure that they heard the message of the gospel in their own language.

Billy Graham's first visit to Britain took place in 1946. He was almost unknown and his team consisted of himself, Cliff Barrows and one other. Eric Hutchings was responsible for him coming, and he had meetings in Swansea, Cardiff, Bristol, Manchester and Newcastle in the six months that they were here. That commenced a lifelong association and Cliff Barrows spoke at Eric's Memorial Service, recalling those days and others.

During his Manchester days Eric was in fellowship at Didsbury from which he was commended in September, 1949 to Edgmond

Chapel, Eastbourne where he was in fellowship for the remainder of his life.

At first Dr. Hutchings worked with British Youth for Christ, but in 1952 he set up his own team under the heading of "Hour of Revival". His methods included radio, crusades, films, tape recordings, gospel broadcasts and a mobile cinema van. The great years for their crusades were in the fifties and sixties when some thirty united crusades were conducted in British cities. Eric's motto was, "No City Too Large, No Town Too Small to Win Souls For Christ". Crusades were also conducted on the continent of Europe, South Africa and the U.S.A.

Lindsay Glegg said about the work of Eric Hutchings' team, "They were the first in Britain to see the value and the possibilities of a weekly radio programme with thorough preparation and follow-up". The Hour of Revival was beamed on Radio Monte Carlo, ELWA Liberia, WIVV Puerto Rico, FEBC over eight stations, to Hong Kong daily, HLKX weekly and on HJCB on Mondays.

Nor was Eric Hutchings interested alone in spreading the gospel. From his early days in Manchester he had appreciated the importance of Bible teaching. He was one of those from three assemblies in North Manchester who commenced ministry meetings on Saturday evenings in a neutral hall in the city centre. The same concern was shown for follow-up with the Hour of Revival. He issued a magazine called "The Hour". He authored a book on Joshua and 2 Timothy entitled, "Training for Triumph". His ministry, and he was no mean Bible teacher, was specially concerned with training believers on how to evangelise.

Eric Hutchings' parish was the English-speaking world. The Eric Hutchings Trust was set up both in South Africa and Australia to do the same kind of Christian service in those parts as he was doing in Britain. Naturally he was a regular visitor to them and both were represented at his Memorial Service.

Eric Hutchings was a man of boundless energy. He didn't only conduct large crusades in public buildings, but he had also a special concern for the lonely and deprived. He wasn't only interested in the spread of the gospel, but he was also anxious about the edification of those whom he saw saved. His wife was Mary Estcourt, whose brother was well-known as the Manager of Plas Menai, the Christian Guesthouse at Llanffairfechan, but they had no children. However their spiritual children were numerous and international.

MARK KAGAN
(1885–1987)

MARK KAGAN

Mark Kagan was born in Riga, capital city of the little Baltic Republic of Latvia, long before that small country was swallowed up in the Soviet Union. There were three synagogues in that city, all served by one rabbi, Mark's father, whose family consisted of three boys and three girls. The boys just had to receive two kinds of education, a religious one and a secular. The religious one was provided at home, but the secular required Mark, in particular, having to go to a school in Bremen for two years. One day, while there, Mark sat opposite a German pastor in a restaurant, and he had a large Bible on the table in front of him. The pastor looked at young Mark for a while, and then addressed him, "Excuse me," he said, "I believe you are a son of Abraham?" Mark replied with, "What has that to do with you?" The pastor responded, "I am very interested because I love the Jews." Mark's retort was: "How can a German pastor love the Jews?" The reply was, "Because Jesus of Nazareth was a Jew, as were the apostles and prophets".

Opening his large Bible the pastor read to him from Isa. 52:13 right through to the end of chapter 53. Mark had never heard that passage read before. The pastor explained that those words referred to Jesus of Nazareth whom he claimed was the Jewish Messiah. Mark couldn't accept that and the conversation ended with the pastor volunteering that he was giving up his church in Bremen and moving to London.

Mark completed that part of his education and in 1902 he too moved to London where he had relatives. (His sisters went to Canada but his brothers remained in Riga where they were eventually murdered when their country was overrun by the Nazis.) Mark settled in the East End of London where there was a large Jewish population. One day he was walking in Whitechapel when he felt a hand on his shoulder. It was the pastor from Bremen who said, "God has put you in touch with me again and I will not let you go." They met regularly for about six months when the pastor led him to Christ. Mark always said, "A Jew led me to Christ and his name was Isaiah."

The pastor introduced him to Gorringe Park House in Mitcham, a Home for about twenty young Jews where he met another Hebrew Christian, J. Yoelson-Taffin, also from Riga. They became lifelong friends working together in Jewish missions. Young Mark attended a church in London pastored by an evangelical who taught him that Jesus was not only the Jewish Messiah, but also Mark Kagan's Lord. As a result he was baptised.

Gorringe Park House belonged to the Barbican Mission through which a large number of Jewish young men were brought to Christ. Mark went to work with that Mission and was put in charge of their work in Whitechapel, where he continued for thirteen years. Later he transferred to the Mildmay Mission to the Jews which was more evangelical. Mark married a Christian lady school-teacher in 1915 by whom he had one daughter. He might have been interned as a foreigner in World War One, but he volunteered for service in the Non-Combatant Corps. He became a naturalised British citizen in 1920.

Workers with the Mildmay Mission received no salary as it was a faith mission and the Lord was expected to supply all the workers' needs. He led many Jews to Christ in those days, but he was not entirely happy with the Mission and he finally left them, venturing out completely on faith to preach wherever the Lord called him.

It was natural for Mark Kagan to have a keen interest in the spiritual welfare of his fellow Jews. Therefore he was for many years Director of the American Board of Missions to the Jews. He was also a frequent contributor to their Yiddish paper, "The Shepherd of Israel". His longest connection with a society was his lifelong membership of the Society for Distributing Hebrew Scriptures which was founded by his friend, Mr. Yoelson-Taffin.

It was in the early 1920's that Mark Kagan sought fellowship with the saints in South Park Chapel in which fellowship he continued until the end of World War Two. From 1945 until 1968 he fellowshipped in High Barnet. The remaining years of his life he was in Berrymede Hall in Acton.

If it is natural for a converted Jew to seek the salvation of his fellow Jews it is equally natural for him to be interested in the prophetic word. It was probably in the inter-war years that Mark Kagan was most busy moving about the assemblies giving addresses on prophecy. The bound volume of "The Believers' Magazine" for 1936 tells about him addressing New Year conferences at Ayr and Kilmarnock on January 1, at Glasgow and Larkhall on January 2, and at Dalry and Newmilns on January 3. He spent a week that same month at Airdrie and another at Overtown in Lanarkshire. The next month, February, he was in Larkhall and Kilmarnock, Glengarnock and Wishaw. He was still in Scotland in March and spoke at the Ayrshire Missionary Conference as well as at Shawlands, Glasgow, at Rutherglen and Blantyre. The only time the writer heard him was when he spoke on Rev. 16 dealing with the way in which the River Euphrates is to be dried up in preparation of a way for the Kings of the East—the only time I have heard anyone speaking on it.

One of Mark's great joys was to visit Palestine for himself before it became the State of Israel. An even greater joy was to point a Jew to the Saviour while he was there, and then at his own request to baptise him in the River Jordan where the Lord Himself had been baptised. That visit added to the list of subjects on which Mark Kagan gave addresses—evangelism among Jews, prophecy and now the Life and Customs of Bible lands illustrated with slides.

In addition to magazine articles Mark Kagan published booklets including "Palestine and the Jew today in the Light of Scripture", "The Certainty and Nearness of Christ's Coming", "The Jewish Passover: How is it Kept Today?" "God and the World Crisis" and "British Israelism Examined by an Israelite".

Service-wise Mark Kagan's first love was the Society for Distributing Hebrew Scriptures. He actually retired from its Council shortly after his 100th birthday, saying, "Now that I am one hundred years and four months old, the Lord has told me that I can retire from the Council. You can do without me now. I am not leaving the Society for I will always be part of this work." Within a few months he had withdrawn his resignation because he couldn't bear to live and not be involved. That Society has sent bi-lingual New Testaments to almost every country in the world. Its motto, and Mark Kagan's was "To the Jew first."

Mark attended his own 100th birthday celebration and spoke for almost an hour without notes on the Messiah in Isaiah's prophecy. He attended one more annual meeting of the Council of the Society for Distributing Hebrew Scriptures at which he pronounced the blessing in Hebrew and spoke with power about the return of the Saviour. Within a week of the next annual meeting, suffering from a slight cold and cough, he slipped off his chair and into the Lord's presence at the advanced age of one hundred and one and a half.

ALBERT LECKIE
(1920–1988)

ALBERT LECKIE

Albert was born into a Christian family in the Lanarkshire town of Coatbridge, brought up in the neighbouring district of Coatdyke, and lived almost all of the rest of his life in the town of Airdrie. His was a godly home with the result that he was saved as early as four and a half years old.

Although topping the class in almost all subjects at school Albert never took advantage of Higher education. At a very early age he was a keen reader of the scriptures, and one of his school classmates, from a different religious background, speaks about the knowledge Albert displayed in the R.E. class in his school days. At home the time was when his father felt that he had to draw his attention to the fact that he was not reading his Bible as much as he might. When the boy remarked that he did not have the same desire to read his father stressed that that was a greater reason for reading. When his father began to think that he was reading too much he suggested to him that he ought to read less and to meditate on it more. Either way the young fellow took his father's advice.

Young Albert left school when he was fourteen and took up a post in a lawyer's office. His employer wanted him to pursue further studies with a view to becoming a lawyer. Albert was baptised when he was fifteen and went into fellowship in Hebron Hall, Airdrie. He seems to have had other desires than pursuit of a profession for he went to "night school" in Motherwell to study Latin and Greek, in the latter of which he seemed to be quite proficient when he was conducting Bible Readings in later years.

Albert loved the scriptures. Eight and nine hours of study per day were not unusual when he was conducting meetings. But he also loved people. His parents' home was a hospitable one. It was always open to the Lord's people day and night. It was suggested that eternity had already begun in the Leckie household for there was no night there. Until his untimely end it was remarkable how little sleep Albert required. This open door applied to strangers as well. During World War Two Polish soldiers were billeted in Airdrie, and Albert would be sent out in the evenings to find such wandering the streets and bring them home for some food and conversation.

In post-war years Albert was manager with a civil engineering company on a hydro-electric scheme in the North of Scotland. One can imagine the behaviour of such a work-force at weekends with plenty of money in their pockets and no opportunity of going home. The local police in Dingwall used to send for Albert on Saturday evenings to get his hard-drinking employees back to the site without trouble breaking out, in view of the respect the men had for their boss. Later on, when he was on the point of embarking into full-time service, accompanied by four young men, he returned on a camping holiday to the district, to contact the men on the schemes with the gospel, distributing a tract written by himself, entitled, "Who Then Can Be Saved?", and conducting open air meetings in the surrounding villages.

Various brethren, like the late Robert Prentice and the late John Cowan, were recognising the young man's gift and encouraging him to consider full-time service for the Lord. Equally he was in such demand for meetings that it became difficult for him to give proper attention to his secular business. Eventually it was the sheer demand for meetings that forced him to leave business.

Albert's great gift was obviously in the realm of teaching, but he loved to preach the gospel. He was more able to mix the two kinds of service in earlier years than in later ones. He and Robert Walker conducted a special series in connection with the opening of the new Gospel Hall in Lossiemouth in 1954. At least five people were saved. During a visit for ministry meetings the next year thirteen young people were baptised.

He had two happy gospel campaigns at Shieldhill, near Falkirk. He hesitated to agree to four weeks of gospel meetings, preaching himself every night, but the Lord helped. Both campaigns in 1955 and 1961 were much blessed. The Gospel Hall was filled nightly, in spite of the fact that for part of the time the snow was six inches deep. It was then that Roy Marshall, now a full-time servant of the Lord, was saved. The second effort was similar to the first and when the Village Hall was taken for the closing meeting it was full. His great joy in the preaching of the gospel was to emphasise the sufferings of Christ. In this connection he would say, "The Lord Jesus endured in three hours what the unrepentent sinner will never exhaust through eternity."

On the personal level during gospel campaigns he showed an acute sense of leading. At Forth, Lanarkshire, another of Albert's happy hunting grounds for both ministry and the gospel, the daughter of his host was under deep conviction but would not yield. Albert could see the concern in her face and wondered if he should take the initiative. The girl had gone to bed, but as soon as Albert popped his head round the door, she cried, "I want to get saved." He was conducting gospel meetings in Innerleven in Fife. A man was showing great interest in the meetings. Albert was travelling by bus which stopped to change drivers where this man lived. As the bus was moving off Albert decided to jump off and call at this man's home although he should have been at his work. He knocked at the door which was answered by the man himself, saying, "I want to get saved." He hadn't gone to work that day because his wife was ill.

Albert's ministry took him to every part of the British Isles and to most parts of the English-speaking world. He was just turned thirty when these visits began. His method was pain-staking exposition. He did not like glossing over passages of scripture. In spite of such detailed method his following was as large as to be almost unequalled. One of his earliest scenes of labour was the North-East of England and his visits there continued regularly until the last. At Warrington the correspondent said that he never failed to draw a crowd. Believers, many of them young, travelled many miles every year to hear the Lord's servant at the London Convention, or at the Eastbourne Readings where for many years he and the late E. W. Rogers, whose close friend he became, conducted the annual Bible Readings at Largs, Ayr, Eastbourne, etc.

One felt that Albert sacrificed home and family for "the Kingdom of heaven's sake." He was very fond of children, but never married. Although his hosts only tended to see him at meal-times, except for the prolonged after-supper relaxing discussions, many of them became his firm friends. He travelled long distances to conduct the marriage ceremonies of their young folk who called him Uncle Albert, and to help them in difficulties, and to conduct their funerals. He was sympathetic almost to a fault.

Albert Leckie's consuming passion was the Word of God. He didn't slow down much after he had a pacemaker fitted. He taught the Lord's people until his last night on earth. He conducted his last meeting at Nantgarw, retired for the night and his host found out in the morning that he was already at home with the Lord. He entered into his rest, the rest which he denied himself here, for the word, "holidays" was not in his vocabulary, and he was known to return gifts that were earmarked for such a purpose.

Dr. GEORGE McDONALD
(1903–1981)

Dr. GEORGE McDONALD

Although an Irishman from Dublin George McDonald, as his name would suggest, was of Scots extraction and may have come from an ex-Glanton Exclusive family. He was saved at the early age of eight while seriously ill, and hearing the doctor say that there was no hope of recovery. However he lived to the old age of seventy eight, although suffering from another serious illness for many, many years.

He was quite young when he was received into the assembly at Bray, and indeed wanted to go to Africa from the time he was ten years old. Even as a medical student he engaged in the Lord's service, helping in open air meetings, which remained a chief interest until the very end of his life. In 1928 he married Eileen Young of Dublin, whose parents had come from Scotland. They were commended to the Lord's work by the assemblies in Merrion Hall, Dublin and Bray in 1930, and proceeded to the Belgian Congo to join Dr. Hoyte in Kabumbulu in Katanga province. He wrote, "We entered the streaming rain-forests of the Congo and began to realise that God had called us to serve Him among the most primitive forest tribes and pygmies where the foot of the white man had scarcely ever trod. We were in the midst of the deepest depths of idolatry and witchcraft, unrelieved by even a glimmer of heavenly light."

"Thirty years later as we were leaving the Congo (now Zaire), we said farewell to twenty three companies of tribesmen and pygmies who were assembling throughout the forests in the Name of the Lord Jesus Christ. From the beginning right through it was the work of the Holy Spirit."

The reason the McDonalds left Zaire was that he had contracted skin cancer. He had been warned by the "dermatological profession" not to return to the high tropics as early as 1947. The rays of the equatorial sun were producing changes in the skin of his head and face, but they continued in the Tropics until 1960. From 1963 he was under constant but intermittent treatment for skin cancer which cautery and deep ray therapy kept in check until 1980.

Retirement from Central Africa didn't mean retirement from the Lord's work as far as George McDonald was concerned. He didn't seek alternative employment. Rather did he look for alternative forms of service in Ireland. His motto must have been, "Occupy till I come" for it appeared in his letters and conversation right until the end. His revised version of that text was, "Occupy, NOT so long as you can, BUT till I come".

With two years to live he wrote in 1979, "Throughout the year our calling of God has clearly been to teach and preach the Word of God, yet continuing in ever-increasing measure to scatter the incorruptible seed, both directly and indirectly." How did he do it?

One way was the witness at the street corner in Dublin every Sunday night. This is how he described it. "The witness continues on Sundays from 8.30 p.m. till 10.00 p.m. They serve in the Gospel singing and distributing 800–1,000 gospel tracts. While they are thus active three or four brethren are sounding forth the old, old story over the amplifier. More than 33,000 thousands of tracts were accepted during the year and many profitable conversations took place. In the wisdom of God some 200 gospels and several Bibles were given to anxious souls. It is our privilege to supply all the literature". Robert McAlister writes, "I can vividly recall him insisting that we stand in the main street of the city at the junction of O'Connell Street and Middle Abbey Street which was virtually 'Preachers' Corner' in those days, and our feet sticking to the ground with ice, but the Gospel had to go forth at all times as far as he was concerned." His insistence was due to the fact that he believed that eternity's history was still being written at the street corner.

That was only one of the directions that the good doctor's service took. He also wrote, "Although there have been severe interruptions in the telephone service, the day and night gospel message, Dublin 764791, has brought the Word of God to many hundreds of people throughout the year. I rubberstamped an invitation to phone this number on every tract distributed in the city and indeed throughout the country. This year's total—40,000."

That letter continued: "... letters by post ..." Esther 8:10. "The prolonged postal strike very seriously interrupted the work of the faithful few who still maintain the vital outreach to the schools, under the title 'Bible Studies Institute'. Many young people, mostly of school age, come to a knowledge of the Holy Scriptures through this service." And another chapter in this amazing story was the annual visit to Croagh Patrick, the 'Holy Hill' 170 miles west of Dublin. He wrote, "As in former years it was our privilege to be on the 'Holy Hill' over the last weekend of July. Approximately 25,000 pilgrims climbed the 2,510 feet steep and rocky mountain, many of them in their bare feet. Five brethren and four sisters took their stand on the lower and mid slopes of the slippery mountain and from early morning offered copies of gospels to climbers. Some 5,000 of these were accepted and over thirty requests were later sent to our office."

So much for the teamwork in which Dr. McDonald was involved. On the personal level he continued witnessing to small and great in the medical, dental and paramedical professions. Every doctor on the Irish Medical Register received a presentable copy of the gospel of John along with two gospel tracts. Every registered dentist was to have received the same by the end of April, 1980. Paramedics and technicians were to receive theirs before the close of that year. He believed that for the majority it would be the first time in their lives that they would have received a portion of God's Word.

Caring on the personal level was another of the doctor's concerns. Their home was used in no small measure for teaching and ministering God's word to many young believers. As for the elderly a vision for a Home for such was born in 1968, but wasn't realised until 1974.

In the later sixties Dr. McDonald was responsible for a radio programme that went out via TransWorld Radio for two or three years. He and Mrs. McDonald were able to pay one visit to Zaire again. Unvisited by any other missonary they found those assemblies continuing in His name. They continued to maintain living links with them until the last.

His wife suffered from a crippling stroke when he was receiving further treatment for his cancer. He wrote, "You will understand

105

how much we value prayerful remembrance as we are confronted with very many alterations in our way of life. Praise God ... I am still able to take a share in witness—public, private, to our wonderful Saviour who said, "OCCUPY TILL I COME." Nine months later the Lord took him home.

TOM McKELVEY
(1896–1983)

TOM McKELVEY

Tom McKelvey of Belfast was both the son and the grandson of evangelists. He was saved after hearing Joe Stewart preaching in a tent on the holiness of God from Isaiah's conversion story in chapter six of his prophecy. He was seventeen at the time and he never looked back.

His first service for his new Master was open air work and tract distribution. A leading evangelical Presbyterian minister tried to take an interest in the young man, offering to have him accepted into the Presbyterian ministry. This encouragement was counterbalanced by ministry given to the Mourne Street assembly by J. H. McKnight who had come to an assembly from the Baptists. Those meetings convinced the young Tom McKelvey that God's pathway was in New Testament assemblies, and so the minister's kind offer was declined. A companion of those days also tried to persuade the young man against baptism and assembly truth, claiming that his spiritual growth would be stunted, and his refusal to accept that advice severed their friendship. Next time they met was in Toronto and to Tom's pleasant surprise his friend was in fellowship with the Pape Avenue assembly there.

Attending the large Easter meetings in Belfast before World War One Tom McKelvey was greatly impressed with two addresses given by eminent servants of God, J. C. M. Dawson and Dr. W. J. Matthews on the judgement seat of Christ. Two addresses on the same subject at the same conference increased the young man's desire to serve God full-time. In 1916 he obtained time off from work to conduct a gospel campaign in Ballinaloob and saw souls saved and added to the assembly there. The next year he obtained leave of absence to conduct a similar campaign in a kitchen at Ommerbawn in County Antrim. Still seeking the signs following of the Lord's approval he joined John Bernard in tent meetings in Cadoxton in South Wales where the blessing was such that the young man could have no doubt about the direction in which the Lord was leading him.

Thus began a life of gospel preaching and ministering to the assemblies that extended to sixty five years without a break. His own experience was used for the guidance of young men who consulted him about serving the Lord full-time. Have meetings, prove yourselves to yourself and others, and watch for the signs following.

Ulster evangelists generally work in pairs and in those early days Tom McKelvey partnered well-known Irish gospel preachers like Joe Stewart and William McCracken. In fact he spent three and a half years with Mr. McCracken in County Armagh, lodging with a lady and her daughter who were members of an Elim Church. Conversations in their home led to them both identifying themselves with an assembly in their home area. The daughter later married Sam Moore and served the Lord with him in South Africa for many years, seeing as many as forty assemblies established among the coloured population. The joint effort of the Lord's two servants, the young and the old, resulted in assemblies being formed in Ballyshiel and Lisnagat. It was then that the younger man went overseas for a few years. He joined Willie Bunting in Canada, seeing blessing in Toronto, Winnipeg and Calgary. Next he spent a summer in tent work with James McCullough in Nova Scotia which resulted in the Debert assembly being formed. After some time in Vancouver he proceeded to New Zealand where he spent six months evangelising with specially fruitful times in Hastings and Napier.

Tom McKelvey was always a gentleman. His bearing impressed many. One Irish elder said about him that he was glad when he turned up at their conference because, even when he didn't take part, you could feel his presence. Similarly after his homecall, the editor of a Canadian magazine said, "If ever there was a man who gave dignity to the work of an evangelist it was Mr. McKelvey." He had a great sense of responsibility and stewardship, and every detail in his life, and home, and service was attended to with meticulous care.

The writer's personal memories of him are first from the season he spent in the Ayrshire Gospel Tent. He spoke like a gentleman, dressed like a gentleman and acted like a gentleman. And his preaching was a teaching gospel. In particular I recall an address on Gal. 4:4–6. Then we spoke together at the Sunday afternoon ministry meeting of the Belfast Easter conference weekend which coincided with Mr. McKelvey's eightieth birthday, when his natural force seemed little abated.

Tom McKelvey expressed the wish that he might preach to the very end of his life. That he was able to do so was made largely possible because Jim Hutchinson partnered him for the last eighteen years of his life. Jim was reluctant to preach elsewhere than in Ulster for most of those years so that the partnership might continue. And so the Lord's servant was in harness to the end. He took a stroke while preaching at Ballywalter and after a few days departed this life, "leaving the world as he had lived in it, with quietness, dignity and peace."

He was often consulted about problems by responsible brethren, who benefitted form his advice, but he never became involved in their problems. He walked at peace with God and with men. His dignity and bearing marked him out as different.

Tom McKelvey was twice married. His first wife died in childbirth, losing the baby as well as herself. His second one bore him no children and predeceased him by many years. Latterly he was very lonely and liked brethren driving him home to accompany him into the empty house. It was then that he stated that he hadn't appreciated fully the loneliness of the evangelist's wife until he occupied the empty house himself. Such was the brother's sensitivity.

Tom is the only known example of a man in Ulster following both his grandfather and father into full-time evangelism. His grandfather, after whom he was called, did this kind of work last century. His father was not a youngster when he took this step in 1916, only two years before his son. Among them they must have given the Lord, Ulster and the assemblies over one hundred years of devoted service.

Mr. & Mrs. CHARLES MARSH
(1902–1988)

CHARLES MARSH

Charles Marsh spent half a century working among Muslims in Africa, wrote a series of popular books, revised the Kabyle New Testament, standardised the Chad Arabic New Testament, and produced an Arabic–French dictionary.

He was born in London in 1902 and went to school in Enfield. His father was a school teacher, and both parents were Anglican. Although encouraged to go to church regularly he never heard the pure gospel. He left school before he was fifteen to become a farmer's boy, and began to attend the Gospel Hall in Chattenden in Kent where there was only one brother in fellowship. Hearing that he required to submit by faith to Jesus Christ as Lord, he went home and in his bedroom thanked the Lord Jesus for dying for him. He was then seventeen and he promptly wrote to every member of his family telling them what he had done. His brother, Donald took the same step, but remained in the Church of England and went on to become Bishop of the Arctic, the largest diocese in the Church of England.

Two months later Charles was baptised. Four months later God called him to work among Muslims. He heard H. G. Lamb report on his work in Algeria. He told of a chief who offered him six palm trees, a ram once a year, and as many eggs as he and his wife could eat if only they would go to his village and tell them about God. Young Charles felt that he could no longer live for self. He worked on the farm six days a week, took a Bible Class on Sundays, preached in the villages of Kent on Saturday afternoons and at least once a week. He started to study New Testament Greek, and study, analyse and note every verse and chapter.

Asking for commendation to Algeria, and Chattenden assembly being so small, he was introduced to elders from three other assemblies to tell them about his call. He was advised to wait, but he continued to prepare himself for missionary service. One brother told him that he would never be able to learn a foreign language.

Finding the way blocked young Charles decided to go ahead on his own. He himself paid the fees for studying at Livingstone College and spent two summers in Gospel Tents with evangelists. At Livingstone he learned medicine, surgery and dentistry and took first place in his exams. Taking private lessons in Arabic, and pursuing the study of Greek he felt that the rest of his time at All Nations Bible College was wasted time. Again seeking commendation and being advised that he should obtain a good position in the world with a view to sacrificing it for the Lord, he wrote to the North Africa Misson and was accepted within a week.

By this time he was engaged to Pearl Lamb, whose father had first interested him in the Muslim world. He left England in 1925 to go to Algeria and married Pearl in 1927. She knew French and Kabyle, so commenced work immediately at Tabarouth, while he learned the languages. Their honeymoon comprised of one day at the seaside.

The Misson sent them to Setif, but they could not find accommodation so they returned to Lafayette where they lived for some thirty six years. The Lord told him that this was to be their part of the great world field. The Kayble people lived in five hundred villages scattered around the field, some of them along a road that rose to almost 4,000 feet high, many of them requiring trekking on foot for four to six hours to be reached. The only way to contact them was to sit where they sat, facing their hardships, eating their food, caring for their sick, listening and sympathising. They were Muslim to the core, yet he had to stay overnight in their homes. He had to witness in their coffee shops and around their mosques. He risked his life in seeking their souls for the Lord Jesus.

Charles increasingly felt the need to establish outstations to reach those villages effectively, but the Mission had neither the vision nor the resources to establish them. He therefore severed his connection with the Mission, just as Messrs. Fallaize and Gabriel had done, and was commended to the work by the assemblies in Bush Hill where he had been born and in

Chattenden where he had been saved and baptised. An outreach was then established at Ourtilane near a large weekly market, providing an excellent centre from which to radiate the gospel. Market days brought crowds of men and boys, regular classes and meetings were established, while on Saturday mornings sick people came from the surrounding villages. He translated the gospels into the local dialect.

The Bible Society realised that the Kabyle New Testament badly needed revised so Mr. Marsh was asked to head the committee. Captain Fiske of Morocco thought that it would be a good idea to have one translation of the Bible for all of North Africa. The Bible Society asked Charles to head the committee of missionaries and nationals to complete the New Testament. This was an impossible task as Pearl and Charles already had twenty–twenty four weekly classes which totally occupied their time.

However Algeria was fighting for independence from France. The French refused further permission to evangelise the villages. The Muslims destroyed every French buiding in sight. The French recovered lost ground and added to the destruction. In 1958 the Marshes took a furlough and returned to a situation that was becoming increasingly impossible when a letter arrived from assembly missionaries in Chad, whose work had been entirely among heathen Africans and who were very conscious that their Muslims had been neglected. The closed doors in French North Africa seemed a good guide to new doors among the same kind of people further south.

Mr. and Mrs. Marsh were in Chad for two years surveying the need, translating the New Testament into Chad Arabic, and giving the Christians the tools they needed for their job—a dictionary, an Arabic hymn-book, several tracts, a booklet entitled, "Share Your Faith with a Muslim" which was published by the Moody Press and ran to seven editions and was translated into six other languages. This work was completed at home. Several lengthy visits were made to both of their mission fields in the next few years while several of his books were published.

After he was sixty five Charles Marsh found a new sphere of service. He called it, "the most thrilling experience of my life". He discovered that he had the gift of reaching young folk. His ministry among them extended to twenty six countries in conjunction with O.M. and its ships, with WEC and others. It was this kind of service among younger people that resulted in his books. "Into Action" and "Ready, Steady Go"—rather surprising books from an elderly man for young folk.

Latterly this great warrior was confined to barracks. Even so he continued to take an interest in his daughter's Kabyle broadcasts in the correspondence from which he got involved.

In early days in Algeria there were years with little reaping. The reaping came with the advent of camps, radio work and correspondence. In addition he never neglected the ministry of prayer which can continue after more vigorous forms of service are beyond our physical abilities. One friend reported that the aged Charles Marsh wanted to know the names of his Bible Class members so that he could pray for them while looking at each of their photographs.

PUBLICATIONS BY CHARLES MARSH

"Too hard for God"—Echoes of Service, Bath 1970
"Streams in the Sahara"—Echoes of Service, Bath, 1972
"Share your Faith with a Muslim"—Moody Press, Chicago, 1975
"Into Action"—STL Books, Bromley, 1979
"The Challenge of Islam,"—Ark Publishing, London, 1980
Others
"The Life of Pearl Marsh", 1981
"Retirement,"—Needleman Printers, London, 1984
"Ready, Steady, Go,"—STL Books, Bromley, 1985

His advice to young people: "Find God's will for your life and follow it whatever the cost."

The essence of Christianity is, "The Lordship of Christ. Christ is Lord."

E

HEDLEY GLOVER MURPHY
(1928–1985)?

HEDLEY GLOVER MURPHY

Hedley was born into a Christian policeman's family. His spiritual lineage was well-known. His mother's family had worshipped and served the Lord in Apsley Street, Belfast for three generations. His mother's uncle was the well-known, eccentric evangelist Frank Knox. Like many an Irish Christian family his parents were anxious to have a missionary in the family, and when Hedley was born they gave him the middle name of Glover from the author of a well-known missionary story, "One Thousand Miles of Miracle in China".

Hedley was one of the many chidren from Christian homes who have been saved through fear of being left behind when the Lord comes. That happened when he was twelve and because his parents were long in coming home from the Prayer Meeting. However young Hedley made little progress in divine things. He tried to hide the fact that he was a Christian and tried to keep up with his school friends. In this frame of mind he left home for his first job—in Belfast. He attended meetings without having much interest in spiritual things until he contracted a serious illness through playing football without being properly clad. He was indisposed for three months with rheumatic fever and St. Vitus Dance. While confined to bed a friend sent him a copy of Dr. Oswald's Smith's book, "The Man God Uses". From that book young Hedley learned to pray with Dr. Smith, "Lord, make me a man after thine own heart". Pronounced fit by the doctor, Hedley said to the Lord, "Thank you, Lord for one hundred per cent health. Now I will be one hundred per cent Yours Forever."

Two weeks later Hedley was baptised in Oldpark Gospel Hall, Belfast and received into fellowship. He came to rely heavily on

God speaking to him through the scriptures. The first such message he got from the Word was, "Do the work of an evangelist" which he fought at first. He then consulted the elders about this kind of work and they put him in touch with an old lady who wanted somebody to run cottage meetings in her home in North Belfast. It was several weeks before any strangers attended those meetings.

About this time Willie Scott of Galloway advertised for young men to spend their holidays evangelising in that corner of Scotland. Three years in a row from 1949 Hedley joined Willie's teams in South-West Scotland in open air and tent work. He thought of joining Willie permanently in Galloway, and was one of about a dozen of those young men who eventually went into full-time service at home or abroad.

Hedley married in 1951 and still had no guidance as to what the Lord wanted him to do. He heard His voice in the story of Joseph standing before Pharaoh when he was thirty years old. Hedley was just twenty five.

How was he to occupy the intervening years? The Lord's answer came in Ballysillan, a new housing district not far form their home. He asked for several sites for a Gospel Hall in that estate before he got one. His elder brethren at Oldpark thought his idea an excellent one but couldn't help financially at that time because of other commitments. After much difficulty in finding who was the owner of the site they got it for a nominal sum. The story of the building of the Hall was a typical story of the Lord providing all the way. In two years the building was ready and the opening conference took place on October 13, 1956 with the veteran evangelist, Willie Gilmore preaching. The next night 200 people attended the first Gospel Meeting. Ninety six children turned up for Sunday School. In the months that followed people, older and younger got saved. The Oldpark elders suggested that it was time to commence "breaking bread" and the first anniversary of opening the Hall saw a new assembly take shape with thirty three believers participating. The first gospel campaign was held the next year, "The Inter-Estate Crusade", reaching out to the estate where the Hall stood, the one where Hedley had had his cottage meetings and a third. The preacher was Noel Flanagan and the Hall was filled nightly.

A couple sought fellowship at Ballysillan who had never been in the Hall. They had been converted through listening to a radio broadcast from Tangier. This encouraged the assembly to listen to those broadcasts and then to wonder if they couldn't do the same from Belfast. Hedley's brother, Jimmy, corresponded with Dr. Paul Freed of Trans-World Radio, and it was agreed that an audition tape would be produced and submitted for approval. Hedley gave the message on that first tape, it was acceptable to TWR and the Irish Gospel Hour was born in 1959.

Hedley was approaching thirty when he believed that the Lord wanted him to leave business and serve Him full-time. His guidance text came from Josh. 1:3 "Every place that the soul of your foot shall tread upon, that have I given you." To Hedley this could only mean that radio wasn't enough, that he must tread the countries being reached personally. In December, 1961 at a farewell Meeting he was commended to the Lord's work. His first opening—in Dublin followed from the radio work.

The Irish Gospel Hour team held crusades in many places. The first and most regular was at Port Stewart each summer. In 1966 that crusade became the Ulster-Scottish when folk from Scotland and England joined the team. The Town Hall was used and the nightly Gospel rally was followed by a Late night extra.

While Hedley conducted gospel campaigns all over the British Isles he was never happier than when conducting united crusades in some big centre.

It was in 1963 that he took a party of Christians to the Isle of Man. Douglas Corporation were very helpful with the facilities offered. The open air meeting on the prom attracted much attention and six hundred people attended the after-church rallies. This was repeated the next year and many souls were saved.

Hedley thought that the day for tents was passed, but he had to use one for his Mid-Ulster Crusades. As many as eight hundred crowded into the Tent with others standing outside. It was claimed that in some way or other the whole province was affected. The campaign was filmed and further blessing was experienced elsewhere when the film was shown.

Hedley was now ready to embark on crusades overseas. His first such crusade was held in Winnipeg in the Civic Auditorium. Other places were visited but the major service was the Winnipeg one. Nineteen seventy one saw him in Bermuda preaching in the Hamilton City Hall and broadcasting both on radio and television.

Hedley had previously led Christian parties overseas but in 1969 he commenced his conducted tours of the Holy Land which deepened his interest in Bible prophecy relative to that land. Also he saw members of his parties getting baptised there.

And so the busy servant of the Lord continued to evangelise and bring souls to Christ. In 1983 he began to feel the strain and eventually suffered a stroke. His old troubles worsened and he was nearly blind. He struggled on hopefully but his work was nearly done. He was not an old man but he had addressed thousands upon thousands, face to face and over the air. He was not blessed with natural children but he acquired a large family of spiritual ones. And those spiritual children are to be found in many places in the United Kingdom and across the Atlantic.

Hedley's autobiography first appeared under the title of "Under His Wings" in 1968. An updated version appeared in 1984 dictated from Hedley's sick bed under considerable physical difficulty.

A. NAISMITH
(1895–1989)

W. F. NAISMITH
(1896–1981)

A. NAISMITH

W. F. NAISMITH

Few families have helped British assemblies more than the Naismiths of Carluke, Lanarkshire. Archie, the elder brother gave thirty six years of his life to India and another twenty at home to Bible teaching before incapacity overtook him. Three of his five sons are well-known Bible teachers, two of them in the U.K. and the eldest in North America. Willie, the younger brother gave fifty years to ministering the Word throughout the U.K. and beyond and his only son has contributed largely to the same kind of service.

Archie and Willie were brought up in a Christian home and in a Stuart party assembly. Their father was employed by the well-known jam-making firm of R. W. Scott of Carluke as was Willie, together giving one hundred and seven years of faithful service to that company. The brothers were brought up with a good knowledge of the writings of J. N. Darby, William Kelly, etc., and with the Little Flock Hymnbook. One of the directors of R.W. Scott was James Scott, author of "After These Things What?" and many pamphlets on prophetic subjects published by the Prophetic Witness Council. Lanarkshire believers referred to that Carluke assembly as "the Scott meeting". James was past his one hundredth birthday when the Lord called him home.

Archie was sixteen years of age before he was saved and several members of his family professed conversion that same evening after a solemn address. He was baptised in 1913 and received into fellowship.

Choosing to be a teacher Archie proceeded to Glasgow University—likely to be the first from a Lanarkshire assembly to do so. His mother had intended to be a missionary but was prevented from becoming one by reasons of ill-health. She therefore dedicated her firstborn to such service and was delighted when he announced that this was his intention. To prepare himself further for this calling he occupied his long vacation between University and Teacher Training College by joining David Ward of Crosshouse near Kilmarnock in a Counties Tent in the Southampton area. A harvest of souls encouraged the preachers to continue in the locality. That explains why he had an English wife, for Alice Mary Cannon was one of the group of keen young Christians who helped the evangelists by distributing tracts and inviting people to the tent meetings.

Both were interested in India. That year, 1919 saw John McCreadie Boyd, a friend of David Ward from his Kilmarnock days, come home on furlough and David informed him of his young colleague's exercise. John put Archie in touch with E. B. Bromley who supervised all our missionary schools in the Godavari Delta, and the outcome was that Archie took charge of the Junior Secondary School in Narsapur. Archie and Alice were married in August, 1922 and set sail for India in November, taking a month on the way of which he kept a detailed diary.

Archie ran that school unitl 1945 when he handed it over to an Indian headmaster. During that time Mrs. Naismith supervised the hostel looking after all aspects of the boys' lives, but Archie Naismith did not just go to India to be a schoolmaster. Not that he achieved nothing of a spiritual nature in that sphere, for many of his lads trusted the Saviour, becoming elders in the Godavari assemblies, and teachers and preachers in other parts of India. While he was a headmaster Archie rose early every morning to study the scriptures and in the evenings he was out preaching, and very much so at weekends. There were around forty assemblies in the Godavari and he visited these throughout the year on a regular basis.

During school holidays cycle tours were undertaken so that Bible teaching might be given against the possibility that one day missionaries would no longer be welcome in the land. In addition short-term Bible schools were arranged at which Indian brethren were instructed in divine things by Messrs. Bromley, Tilsley, Webb, Morrison, Burt and Phair during the daytime with gospel

126

preaching in the evenings. The hot season holidays were taken in the Nilgiri Hills where the boys were at boarding school, but even there Archie would have some preaching to do.

The only rest was on the ship to and from India for furloughs. The time spent at home was a round of meetings. On these occasions his diary was fairly full before he left India for home. At least twice on furlough he was involved in gospel campaigns. For instance he joined Reuben Scammell, an evangelist of whom both brothers became fond because of his visits to Carluke in former days, in a big tent in Cardiff. In 1958, again he collaborated with Robert Walker in a similar effort in Aberdeen.

As mentioned already, the Naismiths had a family of five sons. There was no question of them leaving India for the sake of the family. Some part of the lives of those boys was spent at school on the hills 700 miles away. They did not stay permanently with their parents after they were six years of age. Grandparents in Carluke and other friends took them in. They were burdened about their boys and in a letter dated 1947 they rejoiced that all five were saved and four of them baptised.

Schoolwork, preaching and teaching at home and abroad did not complete Archie Naismith's life work. He wrote articles on devotional and missionary matters for magazines. His brother and he produced joint productions on two occasions. His own works, which ran into repeat editions were "1,200 Notes, Quotes and Anecdotes", "More Notes, Quotes and Anecdotes", and "1,200 Scripture Outlines", the former of which illustrate how methodical was his method of collecting illustrations from his experience and his reading. His historical knowledge came out in his "Pen Pictures of Early Church Leaders" published in India.

But Archie's major literary contribution was for his beloved India. Can we imagine Bible study without a concordance of any kind? The translation of the scriptures into any language is a major contribution to the furtherance of the gospel and of the knowledge of God. Another important contribution is a Bible concordance. Around 1950 Archie broached the subject to missionary and Indian colleagues for the Telugu Bible. Vol. 1 for the New Testament was published in 1963. That was after he had retired from India, and the rest continued during his illness, and with contributions from Willie Morrison, etc., right into the 1980's. His contribution to Vol. 3 from Ezra to Malachi, was the

Minor Prophets. One of the writer's last memories of Archie Naismith was of him propped up in his special bed, legless, correcting the proofs of that Telugu concordance.

After thirty six years in India the Naismiths returned to the U.K. in 1958. Health was one reason for that decision but so also was the need for a teaching ministry, including the need for stirring up more missionary interest. The Smith brothers provided them with a home in Maddiston which they occupied for some twenty years until Alice's homecall in 1979 after much suffering. Archie's health declined and he needed to have both legs amputated. He was lovingly cared for by his sisters in Carluke until they all moved into Auchlochan house at Leshmahagow, from which he was called home in 1989 at the advanced age of ninety three.

His works do follow him. His ministry is being continued by his sons. He was a valued elder statesman consulted freely by the editors of "Echoes" about missionary matters, especially that which concerned India. Until he was quite old he preached with the enthusiasm of a youngster. Until the last a happy man.

While Archie Naismith went off to university his younger brother, Willie followed their father into the jam-making business of Scotts of Carluke. The mother who prayed her firstborn into the mission field to which she had not been allowed to go herself, said to her second son on the day he first set off for employment— "My son, if sinners entice thee, consent thou not." (Prov. 1:10) He never forgot that advice.

When the Government tried to claim Willie for military service in the First World War he registered as a Conscientious Objector and was drafted into the famous 2nd Scottish Company of the Non-Combatant Corps. It was famous for its Christian young men. The fellowship became a training ground for future service. That corps contained at least two future missionaries, P. J. Horne of Bolivia and Alec McGregor of Eastern Europe. From inside family knowledge Jim Hislop described it like this: "It is doubtful if Scotland will ever see the like again. Such a group of Christian young men bound together by sincere conscientious convictions was destined subsequently to leave marks on assembly testimony at home and missionary service abroad. There were not a few future leaders among the Lord's people in that lot. For the rest of their lives they recalled it affectionately as 'our company.' They earned no medals but they earned the Master's 'well done.'"

It was while in the N.C.C. that Willie Naismith met his future wife. He loved to tell the story of preaching one night at a gospel meeting at Kirkliston on Genesis 24:5 concentrating on verse 58: "Wilt thou go with this man?" That evening a young lady professed to trust the Saviour. Two years later he popped the same question and to the same young lady and again she answered in the affirmative—and became Mrs. Naismith.

Remaining in Scotland when Archie went off to India Willie followed his father into the Bible Class leadership in Carluke and continued there until 1935 by which time his name was well-known among assemblies. Moving to Glasgow he joined the Busby assembly which was a better centre for a man who was going to travel as widely without ever owning a car. While he travelled extensively through the British Isles in the Lord's service, preaching and singing the gospel in his lovely tenor voice, as well as teaching the Word he never neglected his own assembly. He commenced a Bible Reading meeting—on a Friday evening when there would be few demands on him for ministry meetings, and later became correspondent for a time.

It is doubtful if any Christian businessman was ever as busy in the Lord's service as Willie, as he was known in Scotland, Fraser Naismith as he was referred to in England. He generally conducted series of meetings—the four Mondays of a month in one place, the Tuesdays in another and so on. Thus the Tuesdays of May were spent at Rutherglen for over thirty years. The weekends of September were spent at Auchinleck for many years—Saturday night being Bible Reading night with Sunday afternoon ministry meetings and Sunday evening gospel ones.

His range of ministry was extensive. His background reading of "early brethren writers" almost complete. He loved to conduct a series on the tabernacle illustrated with a model. He loved the prophetic word and would conduct series based on A. E. Booth's chart "From Eternity to Eternity". But his forte was in the devotional side of the Holy scripture. With what joy he would declare, "The New Testament knows a Secundus (Second), a Tertius, (Third), a Quartus (Fourth), but not a Primus (First). That place is reserved for One alone, the Lord, First, Pre-eminent One."

Or he would preach from Isaiah 42:4 "He shall not fail" asking the question of Acts 8:34; "Of whom speaketh the prophet?" Could it be Isaiah himself, or Moses, or Solomon etc? until all eliminated he could concentrate on his dear Lord. Or again, he would read about the Lord Jesus in Eccles. 5:8 who was "higher than the highest" in the past, in Hebrews 7:26 where He is described as being "made higher than the heavens" at present, and Psalm 89:27 where the Lord Jesus is said to be "higher than the kings of the earth" in the future.

Invitations to give ministry throughout the English-speaking world led Mr. Naismith to take early retirement so that he could respond. He did in 1956 to the regret of the directors of his firm. They thanked him for close on forty five years of service but recognised that he was embarking on "a more important field of activity."

So first in 1956 and again in 1962 Mr. and Mrs. Naismith visited Pakistan, India, Ceylon, Malaysia, Australia, New Zealand, Fiji, U.S.A. and Canada with only three months between the two trips. On various ships he conducted Bible readings for passengers as his brother had done. An Australian magazine described him like this: "A student of the Word, with a grasp of the letter and the spirit of the scriptures rarely equalled, Mr. Naismith possesses the faculty of imparting divine truth in graceful style, assisted by a mastery of the English language. His versatile addresses covered a wide range of subjects, in all of which the visitor appeared at home. The foundation truths of the faith, the doctrines touching on life and godliness, the revelation regarding the church of God, and the call to Christian witness all received able and thoughtful treatment and were heard and enjoyed by many hundreds, not a few of whom testify to blessing received."

In Australia Willie had opportunities for broadcasting on the radio programmes, also recording further gospel messages to be used when he had gone, an opportunity which he never had at home.

In New Zealand R. A. Laidlaw gave him a car to allow him to visit the scattered assemblies in both islands. He took lessons, passed the test and found the car of great benefit. He did not follow this up by getting a car when he returned home. He preferred public transport and said that he had prepared many a sermon in a bus.

The results of these tours gospel-wise included the conversion of a Maori chief and his wife. Also a Scottish sailor who accepted an invitation to the meeting in Wellington at which Willie was speaking. A letter from himself said, "The Lord has given tokens of encouragement in different places, and by these evidences we take courage and go on." Still he felt that the greatest thing he did in the Antipodes was to help ex-Exclusives following the break-up of the Taylor Party. He was consulted by many of them and sought to get them to fix their thoughts on the Head of the church rather than on the church itself.

Returning home the Naismiths decided to settle in Kilmarnock to be near their only son, when they fellowshipped in the Central Hall assembly. He then resumed his U.K. travels. After only a few years Mrs. Naismith who had endured so much loneliness for the Lord's sake, but who had greatly enjoyed their foreign tours, was called home to glory on Christmas Day, 1967. Willie was still able to speak at the Larkhall New Year conference a week later.

Willie was a writer as well as a speaker. He wrote a book on Ruth entitled "Faith's Radiant Path" and a pamphlet on Malachi which took its title from the word, "Wherein?" in the prophecy. He collaborated with Archie in two larger books, "God's Christ and "God's Book" and "God's People and God's Purpose." For many years he conducted the Question page in "The Believers' Magazine" and contributed articles to magazines at home and abroad.

He was always fond of quoting poetry in his preaching and, like his brother he wrote some himself. There is always the chance of these being lost so we append his best-known, a wedding hymn.

O perfect day, with joy anticipated,
When Christ shall take unto Himself His Bride!
With patient grace for this He long has waited
To share the glory with her by His side

The nuptial day—a transcript of the heavenly—
Has once more dawned; and now their vows they take
To love and cherish one another wholly
And live their lives for Christ, the Saviour's sake

May blessings rich and rare abound toward them
As through the busy world their way they wend!
The sunshine of His smile beam ever on them,
These favours from their never-failing Friend!

May peace be their's surpassing understanding,
And grace sustain them all along the way,
With love enjoyed that ne'er shall know an ending
Till Home is reached in God's unclouded day!

He himself reached home on November 26, 1981. His oft-expressed desire was "that I might finish my course with joy, and the ministry which I have received of the Lord Jesus, to testify the gospel of the grace of God."

CHARLES OXLEY
(1922–1987)

CHARLES OXLEY

Charles Oxley's grandparents on both sides separated from "Open Brethren" so-called at the end of last century. One was an overseer and leading brother in Glasgow, and the other in St. Helens. David Oxley of St. Helens married Maggie McGaw of Glasgow and set up home in St. Helens where he was an overseer. Their four children were saved, baptised and added to the church while quite young. However the marriage broke up and when Charles, the subject of our story, was about fifteen the mother and children returned to Glasgow. Here Charles commenced his working life about the commencement of the Second World War, first in a city warehouse and then in the Fire Service.

David Baird, who got to know Charles when he came to Glasgow, described him as having been impressed both by his physical and spiritual stature. It wasn't in his nature to be on the fringe of any group or activity in which he was engaged—he had to be in the thick of it.

One night during an air raid on Glasgow one fireman was missing from an appliance ready to go out on duty. Charles typically took his place, buttoning on his tunic while the engine travelled. As it changed direction Charles was thrown out and seriously injured, the marks remaining with him for the rest of his life. He was expected to preach at Olive Hall, Partick the following Sunday and had been praying that someone would be brought to faith at that meeting. That didn't happen at the gospel meeting, but it did happen in the hospital ward as the result of conversation with a fellow patient. The other job Charles Oxley had was a purser with the Anchor Line.

His secondary education was obtained at Cowley Grammar School and he returned to Merseyside for his university education. He gained an Honours degree in Biblical and Classical Studies, followed by a Mastership for a thesis on the Old Testament.

Mr. Oxley's wife had the same background as himself, growing up in the Needed Truth meeting in St. Helens, after which members of both families kept in touch. She also took up teaching. He had left the Navy and found a teaching post in Alexandria, Egypt where she joined him. Back home she suggested that they might commence a private school, which they did in Tower College, a rambling Victorian building which they bought for a song and transformed into their first school in 1948. This was the first of three schools established by the Oxleys, in all of which they attempted to educate youngsters in a disciplined, purposeful way. When Charles Oxley was called home there were some 1,600 youngsters attending his schools. He became more and more disenchanted with the direction in which state education was going, and wanted his pupils to grow up with a real grasp of Christian values.

But Charles Oxley wasn't only interested in Christian education in Britain. He had first visited India in his sailor days, and went back to it in 1963. Meeting a Christian teacher there he asked him if he had ever thought of founding a Christian school. The Indian Christian teacher admitted that the thought had crossed his mind, so Charles Oxley gave him a ten pound note as the commencement of a fund to establish such a school. Further visits were made to help set up Christian day schools, Bible Colleges and orphanages in North India run by assemblies.

This was not the only cause about which Charles Oxley had deep convictions. He was most disturbed by the moral drift of the British nation. Most of us just deplore this, but Mr. Oxley joined the struggle against the various evils, and indeed led some of those struggles. Instead of just ignoring the misuse of television he joined the fight for its purification. Everybody knows the name of Mrs. Mary Whitehouse, President of the National Viewers' and Listeners' Association. Charles Oxley was its Vice-Chairman. The positive side to this organisation was the struggle to reverse the current, humanist approach to social, religious and personal issues by insisting that the Broadcasting Authorities should fulfil their legal obligations to ensure that nothing was included in programmes to offend good taste and decency, or to incite to crime or disorder. Complaints were constantly made against violence, swearing, blasphemy, sexual innuendo, etc.

At one time he was a member of more than forty organisations concerned with combatting evils of all kinds like the above and homosexuality. The bravest thing he ever did was to infiltrate the Paedophile Information Exchange, even to the extent of becoming its Secretary so that he could expose it. The outcome was that he was principal witness at the Old Bailey trial which ended in the jailing of its leaders.

In the controversy which followed the acquisition of Hamilton College at a throw away price the Scottish press began calling Charles Oxley Mr. Christian. This wasn't because he was always preaching but because he was always denouncing evil, even at its source. He was Chairman of the Campaign for Law and Order, and Chairman of the Merseyside Community Standards Association. For all of these he was a doughty champion and as a result was regularly called on to be spokesman for them on T.V. and radio, especially in his home area. He wasn't so much a champion of good causes as the champion of Christian standards.

Charles left the Needed Truth assemblies in 1958 because he could no longer accept some of their doctrines. His wife and family remained with them for a while longer. He went along to see all four of his family baptised.

After a busy life, because of which he called his wife longsuffering, he was called home at the comparatively early age of sixty-five. His cancer had probably begun when he personally arrested two burglars. He was so quietly spoken that nobody would ever have guessed that he was so courageous.

A. E. PHILLIPS
(1912–1988)

A. E. PHILLIPS

Albert Phillips was born to a farmer/ex-soldier in Dudley Road Wolverhampton in 1912. When he left school he took up employment in a grocer's shop, there being little opportunity for a lad from a working class home proceeding to Higher Education. Out of curiosity he went to a meeting one evening in Tipton Gospel Hall and was wondrously saved at the age of nineteen. His early Christian service was in tract distribution, in door-to-door visitation, open air preaching and text carrying. He seems to have seen results from such Christian service.

Bert, as Albert was known to his friends in Wolverhampton, greatly benefitted from the spiritual atmosphere and deep missionary interest in the old Cleveland Street Chapel in Wolverhampton and a desire to serve the Lord in China was the result. In 1934, at the early age of twenty one, he set out for that vast land with the commendation of the Wolverhampton assembly, and the intimate interest of others in the South Staffs. area.

Bert applied himself to language study and was reckoned among the best speakers of Mandarin. He worked in conjunction with Reg. Vines of Australia based on Seng-mi-Chen in Kiangsi province and they preached the gospel over a wide area. It appears that ancestral homes were open to them and large crowds listened. Due to the unsettled conditions Bert had to return home in 1938.

The time spent at home was put to good account by Bert Phillips. First he took a course at the Missionary School of Medicine in London, which heightened his usefulness in contacting Chinese people with the Gospel. Secondly, he improved his status by taking a wife with a profound knowledge of China and its language, Miss Edith Cuff, who was the daughter of Chinese missionaries.

Thus equipped Bert returned to China with his bride in 1940, living first in Kuling, then Yefing and finally Tienpa. Conditions were no easier, for Japanese invaders were in China. The nearest doctor was eight days' walk away, and the countryside was crowded with refugees. Living close to the Chinese people because of the circumstances, their service was happy, but eventually the political and military situation compelled them to quit. After thousands of miles and miracles, with their first baby Ruth, they arrived in India by plane in 1944.

Nineteen forty six saw them back in China with two children. Their special sphere of service in Nanchang was among students at the National Medical College, but they also had a large Sunday School work and a great outreach to the villages. In six months they distributed 55,000 scripture portions, tens of thousands of tracts and booklets, etc. They had two and a half years of unthought-of open doors before the Communist conquest of the country. But neither the Japanese menace nor the Communist conquest dampened the ardour of the Phillips who simply moved on to Formosa in 1949 after a furlough.

They had a period in Hong Kong and then eight months in Formosa, or Taiwan as it is now called. In Taipei, the capital of Taiwan, Charles Lee, the great Chinese evangelist, and Bert preached the gospel. The response was immediate and appropriate Bible teaching, giving by the two brethren, led to an assembly being formed.

The future of Formosa was threatened by the Chinese Communists and a pressing invitation for two people proficient in the Chinese language to make Singapore their base resulted in a move there in 1950. For the next thirteen years Bert was occupied both in preaching the Gospel and teaching believers in Malaysia. Based in Penang he had a ministry involving Emmaus courses and youth camps as well as preaching and teaching. Many were saved and baptised just as the Lord's servant had seen in the varied spheres in which he had served.

They returned home in 1963 and a wide sphere of Bible teaching opened up for the Lord's servant. They did attempt to return to Malaysia in 1971 but visas were refused in accordance with the Government's policy. They made their home in West Moors in Dorset and Bert moved widely among the Lord's people. He participated in many series of Bible Readings like Largs, Ayr, Aberdeen and Slavanka, etc. Latterly his wife was not fit to go with him, but he was compelled by a heart condition to grind to a halt, going home to glory in 1988, having left his mark on several countries of the world, never allowing any obstacle to stop his participation in the Lord's service.

"Every conversion to Christ is a miracle, for it is 'of God'. As the Lord stated 'with man it is impossible'. Besides being a miracle it is also a mercy, for it is of the Lord's grace. The call to serve the Lord is a further mercy, (2 Cor. 4:1), and any reward in the future will be of mercy too." Bert Phillips insisted that the scriptures referred to, very much applied to him.

ARNOLD PICKERING
(1908–1984)

ARNOLD PICKERING

Arnold Pickering was a third generation Christian, but had none of the weaknesses associated with the third generation. His father and grandfather comprised two of the four brethren who commenced the Hope Hall assembly in Manchester, one of the first in the city. Arnold was one of a family of thirteen who were brought up in Hope Hall.

Arnold's father, Thomas moved to Stockport in connection with his accountant's business and met with believers in an old billiard hall. Moving house he also moved assemblies, helping to commence a new one in Crescent Road. Arnold, like many another, could not recall the exact date of his conversion but was sure enough about it having happened and so was baptised when he was twelve years of age. From then on, for the rest of his life he was in fellowship in that assembly—a one assembly man, a situation which is becoming much less rare than it used to be. Here he participated in service, here he married Elsie Jones whom he had known from Sunday School days, and here he became a leader which role he occupied for many years.

Arnold's influence on young folk was immense. They welcomed the young folk from the assembly into their home for a weekly Bible study and this continued over many years so that the whole of the New Testament was covered and selected parts of the Old. This kind of service extended to other young folk for previous to World War Two brethren from the N. Midlands asked him to be secretary for a residential conference for young people. It commenced in 1940 and continued until 1972. Many young prospective missionaries attended this including Stephen Downs, Albert and Wendy Gray, Dorothy Hall, Joyce Shackley, etc. Out of this annual conference others sprang and Arnold became involved in the Wessex conferences, and in the Young Men's

Bible Teaching Conferences.

Nineteen thirty nine was an interruption to all sorts of normal life in the major countries of the world. Arnold Pickering exercised his right to register as a Conscientious Objector and so had to appear before a tribunal. The Tribunal ordered him to take up hospital service, but the Ministry of Labour overruled in view of the administrative work his firm, in which he had joined his father, was doing for local organisations.

Arnold's first contact with "Echoes" took place in 1955 when he called at Widcome Crescent on another matter. At the end of the next year he received a unanimous invitation from the existing editors to join them in their work. Various circumstances prevented him accepting at the time, one being the receipt of a similar invitation to join another long-established Christian work on a full-time basis, and another the education of his son. Perhaps more than all was his love for his own assembly in which he was so immersed with his wife, plus the personal nature of his business because of which he did not want to let long-standing clients down.

He did not join the editors until 1959, nor did he leave Stockport then, but travelled to Bath as required. His administrative responsibilities among assemblies were increasing at about the same time. In 1955 he became trustee of "The Harvester", in 1958 a Director of Stewards Company Ltd., and a trustee of the Muller Homes for children. After joining "Echoes" he became a director of Continental Lands Co. Ltd., and Secretary of the Laing Trust in 1964.

He did travel widely ministering the word and reporting on "Echoes". He lectured at Capernwray on the Sermon on the Mount for years and after he had been with "Echoes" for twenty five years his colleagues honoured him by publishing these talks in a book called "The Radiant Life" which he exemplified in his living. It was in the residential scene that Arnold Pickering shone. On such occasions he gave what he called "pillow talks" which dissolved fears and doubts. His stock of stories was immense and he used them to relax folk at meals and bedtime, etc.

At "Echoes" he had the reputation of being a peacemaker. It was he who could disarm and pacify. He lost his partner in 1972 after a period of ill-health during which Elsie was anxious that he should not cut down on the Lord's work. He married Doreen, his

144

secretary at Bath some two years later and she became well-known as she travelled with her husband and nursed him during his long, last illness.

ALEC PULLENG
(1897–1986)

ALEC PULLENG

There is a strong missionary bent in this volume, not only because of the fair number of missionary giants whose stories are told, but also because of the homecalls of a number of brethren who gave their time and talents in the service of missionaries. Among them we must include Alec Pulleng who was a giant in the obtaining of missionary information.

Alec was born into quite a poor family in the Hackney district of London in 1897. While his mother was a church-goer his father was politically active. However Alec was sent along to Sunday School in Paragon Hall, the third oldest assembly in London. He was converted there when he was sixteen and there too he was baptised and received into fellowship.

Like others of his generation he could not have anything other than elementary education. Study by correspondence was the means of him getting into the Civil Service. For his Bible study he used the local reading room. Very early in his Christian life he learned the value of study and of "redeeming the time." He said, "Saturday afternoons are too valuable to be spent watching football." The Lord's work provided ample opportunity for putting these afternoons to good use.

Conditions at Paragon were almost ideal for a willing young Christian. They had three couples on the mission field so that missionary interest was strong. Then the young men were being called to the forces at the beginning of World War One with the result that a keen young fellow had plenty of opportunity for early initiation into Sunday School teaching and other assembly responsibilities.

He enlisted in the Royal Navy Air Service in 1916 but was given an office job under a Christian, and he was off duty at weekends which gave him many free weekends to be at Paragon

Hall. He saw every move as a step further into the divine mould for him. He became a man of single purpose, having little time for recreation, small talk or light reading. At Paragon he met a likeminded partner, who was very much involved in the things in which he was interested. His joint involvement in assembly activities with Nellie Ginnings resulted in their marriage in 1920.

The young couple agreed that Alec would not go in for further study to improve his career prospects but would be content with Alec holding a humble job in the Ministry of Labour so that he could devote all his spare time and energies to the Lord's work. He loved missionary biographies and stored his mind with their contents so that he could illustrate his addresses.

Just after World War One the Missionary Study Class movement began among U.K. assemblies, and the Pullengs were involved from the first. These were designed to interest assembly youngsters in the mission field. The first London one was held at Easter, 1920 with Alec as Joint Secretary, which position he held until he was evacuated at the commencement of World War Two. In addition he participated in such Conferences around Britain. For a time they thought of becoming missionaries in Spain and contacted W. E. Vine for advice. They never received definite guidance so they never went. However he kept increasing his missionary knowledge and contributed to "Links of Help" and other magazines on missionary matters. This information was often obtained from the missionaries whom they entertained in their home, and it was shared with the young people who met in their home and with missionary study groups.

During this time Nellie developed serious eye trouble which eventually led to her blindness. It was painful in the extreme, but she would not let it hinder her husband in his life of service. They were evacuated with his Government department when World War Two commenced to Southport. Needless to say he was as much involved in assembly matters there as he had been at Hackney. Here too they suffered the biggest sorrow of their lives in the sudden death of their only son, two days after his eighteenth birthday. His ministry of comfort, enhanced by Nellie's homecall in 1957, resulted in his first book, "Sorrow turned to Joy."

With the end of World War Two the Pullengs returned to London to become more involved than ever in missionary matters. The desire was to increase the size of "Echoes" so that surveys of mission fields could be included. Bureaucracy would not allow an increase in the size of "Echoes", but could release paper supplies for a new magazine which took shape as "Echoes Quarterly Review" which continued as a separate publication until it was incorporated in "Echoes" itself in 1979. Alec Pulleng was the editor for all of that time.

In 1947 his life of service and his caring for Nellie made Alec consider giving up employment and devoting himself entirely to the Lord's work. Her illness finally enabled him to take early retirement in 1950 and, at last, they removed to Bath, where they had been wanted at "Echoes" for so long, W. E. Vine having recently gone home to glory and W. R. Lewis being very frail. In addition to being an editor of "Echoes" he was a director of Stewards Company Ltd., and a member of the council of the Retired Missionary Aid Fund and of the Widows and Orphans of Missionaries Fund.

Wherever he lived, Alec Pulleng played a large part in the life of the assembly—Hackney, Southport, and now Bath. It was now, to some extent because of the encouragement of Sir John Laing, as he later became, that the editors began to visit missionaries on the field. This encouraged missionaries in all their loneliness and increased the editors' appreciation of their work and their problems. In Sir John's company he visited N. Africa, Spain and Portugal in 1952.

It was in 1957, the year after Nellie's homecall, that Alec's second book appeared. It was a successor to W. E. Vines, "Divine Plan of Missions" and was entitled "Go Ye Therefore". It was written on the assumption that Christians who believe that the scriptures are a complete guide for their worship and service, are equally a complete guide for their missionary work.

"Echoes of Service" was 100 years old in 1972. It was Alec Pulleng who conceived the idea of a volume to celebrate that important date. Each of the editors was given an area to survey and describe and he chased the rest until its completion. So "Turning the World Upside Down" came into existence and about 11,000 copies have been sold. It is a mine of information about assembly missionary work, a veritable encyclopaedia.

Alec married Annie McArd of Southport in 1959 and they moved to Bognor Regis in 1966. In a sense it was the beginning of Alec's withdrawal from "Echoes". He commuted for the editors' meetings, and kept in touch by telephone. Once more he became involved in the local assembly's activities. The writer's first meeting with him took place here as he stood at the door on the Lord's day morning, and as he examined our letter of commendation he remarked, "Oh Annbank! I know your missionaries." Here he fell asleep in 1986 at eighty nine years of age, never a missionary in our sense of the word, but a missionary statesman, and a great helper of the missionary cause.

TOM REA
(1890–1980)

TOM REA

Tom Rea was born into a Christian family in the Ulster town of Lurgan, and therefore knew about his need of a Saviour from his earliest days. That need was met when he was still young. Early in his Christian life he showed an interest in spiritual things, becoming involved in gospel work in neighbouring towns and villages, and in serious study of the scriptures.

He also had an interest in missionary work which resulted in him being commended by two Belfast assemblies, Victoria Hall and Ormeau Road to Central Africa in 1911 when he was just twenty one years of age. He accompanied Mr. and Mrs. Cunningham as they returned to Kalunda in Angola. Although Tom was not among the first wave of assembly missionaries to Africa things were still primitive. The journey took seventy one days, much of it on foot. By river barge, propelled by natives, and on foot, single file along nine inch wide paths through the forest, they finally arrived at their destination and then took up residence in clay and wattle huts with dirt floors, slept on beds made of sacks filled with chaff, and ate local produce all the time.

The young man so far from home buckled into language study until he became an expert in Lunda, and engaged in pioneer gospel work in the villages around. He went on furlough in 1917, and on his return found that Ethel Isherwood from Manchester had arrived during his absence. He chose to marry her the next year and so began over fifty years of service together in the heart of Africa.

In 1923 the Reas moved across to Congo, now called Zaire, and joined Jack Prescott and his wife at Tshiwilu. The two men were evangelists and there was much blessing in the district. Ordered to move on by the Belgian Government they went to Nyanama for the next three years. All the time Tom Rea was translating. Instead of sending his translated scriptures back home for printing some friends sent him a printing press to Africa. It required a hundred men to move it, but good use was made of it, producing each book of the Bible on it, as Singleton Fisher and himself turned them out. His son, Eric can recall his dad being locked up for hours daily with Manase and one or two others in the painstaking work. Messrs. Rea and Fisher translated and revised the Lunda Bible as well as translating many hymns and other literature into that language.

Tom Rea was to become an accomplished linguist. He learned to speak French, Lunda, Zovale and Chokwe. After three years at Nyanama they went to work among the Chokwe people on the Congo-Anglo border at Dilolo. It was to become an important railhead in later years but long before that the Reas were to see the greatest work of their lifetime take place in it.

The Reas succeeded in getting home to Ireland in 1942 during the Second World War, and had to stay at home for its duraton. Afterwards they returned to Africa, but to Zambia, as it is now called. He now became noted for his Bible teaching both among native Christians and among fellow missionaries. And this reputation extended over the border to Angola, to which he made several extended visits, and gave ministry which was remembered for a long time, according to Ernest Wilson who listened to him appreciatively then. He was also able to visit his son, Eric, who, with his wife were medical missionaries in Kerala, so that Indian missionaries too were able to derive profit.

But Mrs. Rea's health was deteriorating so they left the Tropics and served the Lord in South Africa for two years. Everywhere his ministry proved helpful. A return home became necessary, but it was made via the U.S.A. where his daughter lived after she and her husband, Mr. J. Bell retired from the teaching staff of Sakeji School for the children of missionaries. So brethren in yet another continent had the opportunity of sampling Tom Rea's ministry. The third member of their family Darrell stayed on in Africa, a businessman with a deep interest in the Lord's work. His son, William was to give a number of years to missionary service, also in Zaire, before returning to England for his family's education.

Shortly Mrs. Rea was called home to glory. After some time Tom married Mrs. Johnston, who provided him with a home base for his remaining twelve years, from which he could continue his work of Bible teaching, in Ulster in particular. A man of another generation, Derick Bingham, in his magazine for young people called, "Think", urged his young readership to take the opportunity of hearing Tom Rea ministering the Word of God if they could, because it was Bible teaching at its best.

His fellow-Irishman Ernest Wilson described him like this: "Mr. Rea was a typical Ulster Christian gentleman. At times he could be blunt in his remarks with a mixture of Irish humour and quick repartee. He had no use for hypocrisy or pious humbug, and he could deflate a snob with a few well-chosen words. At the same time he was one hundred per cent an assembly man and loyal to the core to the person of Christ and His Word."

DUNCAN REID
(1897–1985)

DUNCAN REID

Duncan Reid was born in Motherwell into a Christian family in 1897. He was converted at sixteen years of age and immediately became involved in Christian work in Roman Road Gospel Hall. In 1920 he emigrated to Canada and while there he met A. Peterkin, on furlough from the Argentine, had been so impressed with the description of the terrible spiritual need of the Rome-dominated Dominican Republic that he was going there instead of returning to South America. Duncan decided on the same path and in preparation spent some time at a Bible School in New York in 1920, returning to Scotland to get married in 1921. His bride was Mary Campbell of Irvine, daughter of a leading Ayrshire brother of the time. Her sisters married John McAlpine, a much-used evangelist in the U.K., and Peter Horne, who became a missionary to Bolivia. Duncan and Mary set out together for the Dominican Republic that same year.

Their first task was to learn the Spanish language. It was then felt that the Reids, along with the Moores who had transferred from Guiana, should commence a new work in Puerto Plata on the north coast of the island and very near the spot where Columbus had landed in the New World some four hundred years before. Conditions were difficult. If buildings were obtained for the work the missionaries would soon have to vacate them. During the first year three souls were saved, but there were no more conversions during the next five years. It was 1930 before they were able to obtain their own building, and then things began to happen. That hall could accommodate two hundred and twenty people, but it had to be extended in 1935 to seat between four hundred and five hundred. The Reids decided to put great effort into Sunday School work which is not easy in a Catholic country. Sunday School commenced with three little girls and, as with adults, growth was slow, in five years only twenty five were attending. Progress improved after the new hall was obtained and by 1950 there were five Sunday Schools with a total roll of over 1,000.

But the Reids did not concentrate on Puerto Plata alone. They reached out to the villages, travelling on horseback as there were no roads. Eventually there were twenty assemblies in the Puerto Plata district and around the north coast. Duncan recalled those days on horseback when along that north coast he would not meet a single Christian, and compared the situation after their sixty years in the area when there were fifty two assemblies.

In 1938 Duncan and Ian Rathie saw the immense possibility of radio work. A small radio station opened in the town and the owner offered to broadcast the Sunday evening service at a ridiculously low price. The station was heard in the neighbouring islands, and as it became more powerful people could hear it in much of Central America. One of the greatest thrills was the conversion of a Roman Catholic priest from Venezuela. He bought a radio in New York and was searching for an interesting programme one Sunday evening when he tuned into the service from Puerto Plata. He listened in secret for weeks, afraid that anybody would get to know. After two years he trusted the Saviour as he knelt beside his radio. He went to Puerto Plata, found the Gospel Hall, and realised that the preacher was the same to whom he had been listening on the air. He had to leave the service early, but returned later to tell Duncan about the miracle of conversion and his resignation from the priesthood.

A daily paper carried an article by a lawyer who expected the Roman Catholic church in the town in the interior to be packed on a Saint's day, but it was not. In the evening he wanted to hear the news bulletin and learned that there were only two radios in the town, one at each end. He went in search of one of them and discovered a crowd outside—listening to the service from Puerto Plata. Disgusted he walked to the other end of the town and found the same there. His article called on the priests to wake up or all of those country places would be converted to protestantism.

The radio work grew. Eventually there was a fifteen minute programme entitled "Beginning the day with God", a Saturday one for half an hour, plus the live one each Sunday evening. This last continued to be the most popular and Duncan Reid claimed that several country assemblies were the direct result of the radio work.

As happened to a number of missionaries who remained on the mission field during the dreadful days of World War Two Duncan was asked by the British Government to be Vice Consul. This enabled him to do a lot of work among ship-wrecked sailors from torpedoed ships in the Atlantic, for which service he was honoured with an O.B.E., the first of several honours conferred on him. Before his homecall the freedom of Puerto Plata was conferred on him in a town which had grown considerably since 1924, now being a busy tourist resort and boasting of an international airport.

In the early days a small kindergarten school was commenced in the town. In 1960 a number of Christian school teachers expressed concern about the state of the local schools, and suggested the setting up of a Christian one. Duncan gave the idea his blessing but insisted that it be self-supporting. It commenced with seventeen pupils and the teachers were content to divide the income after expenses were paid among themselves as their only recompense. From those small beginnings it has grown until it has almost one thousand pupils and disadvantaged children are taken in on being sponsored by Christians elsewhere.

More children's work has been done in the post-war period through Daily Vacation Bible Schools during school holidays. Thousands of children are reached each summer as they return to school during their holidays for a fortnight at a time of Bible lessons and handwork.

Nor did the Reids neglect Bible teaching and pastoral work. Duncan was always anxious to give consecutive Bible teaching, while Mary was a keen visitor. Shortly after the War, to help native brethren develop gift in evangelism and Bible teaching a five day conference began. At the beginning the speakers were the missionaries but gradually local gift was recognised and the missionaries ceased to take a prominent part.

In the mid-seventies Duncan came home to Britain with a serious condition. Cancer resulted in the amputation of a leg right to the hip. The last time the writer saw him was when he was convalescing in his daughter's home in Leeds. It seemed impossible that he and his wife would ever return to the island.

But he did.

Mr. Reid recalled that during his first furlough at the London Missionary Meetings he met a veteran missionary and asked him if he was retired. His answer was, "My boy, true missionaries never retire." In that spirit Duncan returned to the Dominican Republic and added another ten years to his life of service. His father was still preaching in Canada at one hundred years old. The son was doing it in the Dominican Republic at eighty eight, after spending sixty four years in his Master's service there. Mary's mental condition did not allow her to remain in the West Indies, and she was brought home to be cared for by Muriel in Leeds, continuing life till 1989.

A fellow-missionary, J. R. Cochrane edited a biography in Spanish of Duncan Reid and included some of his addresses in it.

Mr. & Mrs. WILLIE REW
(1886–1984)

WILLIE REW

William Ritchie Rew was born in the Angus village of Strathmartin, the son of a textile mill owner, in 1886. He was one of ten children whose parents were not saved when they got married. Their conversion changed their lives completely, family worship being commenced in their home, and regular attendance at the assembly in Hillbank Hall, Dundee, four miles away on foot. It was during family worship one Sunday evening, that young Willie, until then not interested in spiritual things, heard God's voice whispering to him: "This is your last chance. If you do not believe now, you will not have another chance." He responded immediately, and never looked back. This happened when he was fifteen years of age. Baptism followed at the Dundee New Year Conference shortly afterwards.

From the beginning the youthful Willie Rew loved the scriptures, loved to pray and loved the assembly gatherings. A brother who took a keen interest in young Christians, gave him his first opportunity to take part in a meeting by inviting him to open a Saturday evening meeting. He got up, read his passage, gave out a hymn, prayed, said "If you get as much out of this scripture as I have, you will do well," and sat down.

Willie's missionary interest was fired by hearing Dr. H. Grattan Guiness at Keswick. Back home he became Secretary of a new Missionary Study Class. This led to his defininte commitment to missionary work.

The family moved to Perthshire. Father and son were joint founders of the new assembly in Doune. The mill in which they were involved still stands today—a conserved building. Several members of the Rew family have left their names inscribed on it.

The First World War saw Willie Rew move to Clydebank where he worked in the famous Singer's sewing machine factory.

The war postponed any possibility of travelling to any mission field. Meantime he was introduced to Margaret Smith from Ayr. It was love at first sight and they were engaged three weeks later. She said later that she would not have married him if he had not been interested in missionary work.

In Clydebank the young man helped to plant a second assembly, the one which meets in Victoria Hall. Here too their first baby was born, and the brethren were reluctant to commend a young couple to Africa in case their new baby would be unable to live in that inhospitable climate. Willie preached the gospel round Glasgow area. The writer remembers having supper in a Christian Guest-House in Ayr with two elderly Christian ladies and Gordon and Margaret Jones, when one of the ladies asked Margaret if she was Willie Rew's daughter. When Margaret replied in the affirmative the lady responded "My sister and I were saved when your father came over to preach the gospel in Johnstone." From Clydebank they moved to Norwich for war work i.e. the building of aeroplane bodies. It was here they were living and from which they were commended in 1921, after a year at the Missionary School of Medicine in Great Ormond Street.

The way to Africa did not open until Mr. Rew was a mature man of thirty five. Communications in that continent were not as poor as in the days of the pioneers. Still beyond rail-heads new missionaries had to trek into the interior. It was a three week walk, Mrs. Rew being carried in a hammock while her husband walked. Their belongings were carried by native carriers. They camped out every night in this strange land with its strange climate. They were heading for Kalunda to join Tom Rea of Ulster whom they had met in the homeland while he was on furlough. He had been in Kalunda since 1911, but when they discovered that quite a number of new missionaries; held up at home because of the war, had gone to Kalunda, they went to Kavungu instead. The next twenty months were occupied learning the language of the district. It was when Mrs. Rew was returning to Kavungu after the birth of Kathleen, later Mrs. Dudley Dalton, that one of the carriers asked, "Why don't you go where people have not heard the gospel?" Mrs. Rew asked him where such people were and the result was that Dilolo appeared on the missionary map.

Imagine living with a growing family in a place six hundred

miles from the nearest shop, where goods like flour, sugar, tea, paraffin, etc. could be obtained. And these could only be obtained in the dry season when the journey occupied three months there and back. One year they had no money for the yearly shopping list so the trip did not take place. However a caravan of thirteen men arrived carrying loads which were deposited at the Rew's door. These supplies had been sent from a prospector to whom the Rews had previously given hospitality when he had taken ill in the district. Now employed he bought a year's supplies for the Rews when he was purchasing his own.

Other items that we would consider essentials were not known to the Rew children while in Africa. They never wore shoes and furlough was looming up. Anna in particular had none. In answer to prayer a man appeared offering to sell them a pair of girls' shoes which he had bought at Elizabethville five hundred miles away, and now in need of money he offered to sell them. They were a perfect fit for Anna.

The natives were a long time in understanding the gospel. The first convert was a fifteen-year-old lad who stood up in a meeting and said, "I want to believe in the Lord Jesus". He went on to become a preacher and an elder in a meeting and served the Lord for fifty years. From then on the work grew but the Catholics arrived and planned to cover the district with schools. A battle ensued, the Catholic authorities leaning towards Catholic schools but the people wanting Mr. Rew's schools. Three hundred were built in three months and he had to find teachers for them. He visited Angola to see if teachers could be obtained there and returned without having achieved success.

He then found that the workers laying the new railway line were having Christian services. They turned out to be Lubans who had been carried off as slaves and had been converted in slavery. Now that slavery was abolished they had the liberty to return to Lubaland, but hearing of the need for teachers they stayed on at Dilolo to fill the gap.

Mr. Rew's first means of transport was a bicycle, and when he eventually got a truck they had to build eighteen miles of road for it. Many a tale could be told about the problems of negotiating African bridges with that truck, and with a later car, including the occasion when the bridge broke and Mrs. Rew was tossed into the river and carried some distance downstream.

After twenty three years in Dilolo the Rews had seen some three thousand people trust the Saviour. Sixty of them had become teacher-evangelists, full-time servants of the Lord. They had seen many meeting-places erected in the Bush.

The Rews had to take one of their sons to Elizabethville for medical attention. There they met hundreds of believers who had been attracted to the town for work. The only church was Methodist but they greatly missed the practice of believers' baptism and the weekly breaking of bread. They had appealed to other missionaries for help without success and now they appealed to this sixty-year-old. There were enough missionaries, including his own family to carry on in Dilolo so the new challenge was accepted.

The big obstacle was that buildings in Elizabethville would have to conform to a reasonable civic standard, not the make-do situation of primitive parts. And all of this was going to cost a deal of money. Initially they took a disused hotel ten kms. out of the town and this was their first home in the new locality. It was so run-down that the family did not want their school mates to know where they were living.

However the Lord took a hand in what was going on. First a retired postal official from Pretoria sent £100 when he heard of the new project. A fellow-missionary, with characteristic missionary generosity sent £60. Then John Laing arrived to discuss the Luba translation of the scriptures and announced that he and his wife were giving £1,000, later increased to £2,000. A further £1,000 arrived in the mail. Thus a meeting-place for the first African assembly in a city was provided and on the first Lord's Day four hundred and fifty commended Africans gathered to remember the Lord.

Mr. and Mrs. John Duff of Chicago were visiting Africa and were shown hospitality by the Rews. A violent thunder storm put out the lights and showed that their home was very leaky. Elizabethville was central for many missionaries in Central Africa. The Duffs decided to make it possible for Restawhile to be erected, not just a home for the Rews, but a home from home for travelling missionaries. Moreover the area was evangelised and by the time of the Katanga war and Willie Rew was ninety one there were some forty assemblies in the area, only three of which had been there when they came to the district.

The political situation was deteriorating and Mr. Rew was increasingly crippled from injuries sustained when his car overturned away back in his youth. With roaming soldiers who were little better than brigands, it was increasingly difficult for the others to have a care for him when danger was near. Mrs. Rew was called home in 1963. Undaunted Mr. Rew carried on with the work and eventually married one of the lady missionaries from Chamfubu, Win Wagland.

Win looked after him well. Willie was not very mobile but ran Bible School on Saturdays to prepare natives for future leadership, until the Government required them to give part of their free day for public works. When son Willie had his face badly smashed by a brick thrown at him, it was apparent that it was better for the old warrior to come home. It would have been delightful if he could have remained in Zaire as one whom the African believers could consult. He made his home first in Renfrew and loved to visit the different assemblies on Lord's Day mornings, Doune in particular, where Dr. and Mrs. McColl, formerly of Zaire, had settled. At the ripe old age of ninety eight, in spite of fifty seven years in the Tropics, the Lord took him home from Auchlochan House, Lesmahagow.

In more ways than one "his works do follow him." Three daughters married missionaries in Africa, while son Willie still carries on faithfully in Katoka, Dilolo province with his wife, Cathie. Three of the Jones' sons are in the Lord's work with their partners, Deryk and Sandra in Zimbabwe, Rodney and Deborah in Italy and Leslie and Sharon preparing to serve the Lord. Three of Elizabeth's family, the Wilsons, are also serving the Lord.

Joy and husband Darrell Peters are in the border between Zambia and Malawi and Darrell accompanies his cousin-in-law, Deryck Jones on his regular visits to Malawi to encourage the new assemblies there which have no missionaries of their own to guide them. Anne and husband, Richard Hoyte, also of missionary parentage, serve the Lord in Chad, while Jacky and husband Neville help at Sakeji school in Zambia where she used to be a pupil.

JOHN R. ROLLO
(1905–1981)

JOHN R. ROLLO

Like Timothy and a good many more of us John Rollo was born into a Christian family and therefore "from a child knew the holy scriptures which were able to make him wise unto salvation." The result was that he was saved as a boy of twelve in 1916. Like so many of us in Ayrshire, Lanarkshire and Fife his father was a miner and he grew up among miners. Nevertheless he was able to take advantage of secondary education and even at this stage in life young John took his stand for God.

Proceeding from school in Buckhaven, John went to St. Andrews University, leaving home for the first time to lodge in that old Scottish town which he came to love. Naturally his faith was tested there but he came through with flying colours. He loved the university town and took great delight in showing it to his friends for the rest of his life. He took a keen interest in the little assembly, even as a student and when the demands of study would have suggested that he stay at home on meeting nights, the needs of the little company of the Lord's people took him out.

John graduated with a second class honours degree in English and History and entered the teaching profession. First he taught in Beath High School, Cowdenbeath, moving from there to Viewforth Junior Secondary School, Kirkcaldy, first as Principal Teacher and then as Headmaster. Those familiar with the system that obtained will understand that promotion was decided by County Councillors of political persuasions. Canvassing was officially forbidden but generally continued with the encouragement of some councillors at least. John Rollo had some unsuccessful interviews for headmasters' jobs and one councillor said to him, "Rollo, you'll have to lecture them". John's principled reaction was: "Should I never". In the event John was rewarded with the headship of his own school, which was fairly unusual. In education John Rollo was highly regarded. He was mainly responsible for a widely-used series of English text-books. For many years he chaired the Examination Panel for the Primary to Secondary Transfer Exam. He did much for the development of Junior Secondary Education.

And his interest in young people didn't stop at school. For most of his days he was very interested in the spiritual welfare of young folk. He was actively involved in the teaching side of the Fife Bible Class Camp, one of the first Christian Camps in Scotland. For some fifty years he was involved with Scottish assemblies' Conventions at St. Andrews, then at Netherhall, Largs, back at St. Andrews from 1945–1948 and then at Aberdeen from 1948–1951. There were later occasions again at Netherhall, after one of which a booklet was published containing John's ministry on Discipleship. Many were influenced by the ministry given at these conventions and at his funeral Jim Hislop testified to the effect that Mr. Rollo's ministry had had on him at one such convention, leading to a change in the direction of his life and a lasting friendship with the man whose ministry had had such an effect on him.

His ministry was, of course, wider than that. From Aberdeen to London, and from Edinburgh to Belfast John Rollo carried heart-warming ministry to the Lord's people. Edmund Ewan described him as an artist in words who is remembered among the assemblies for his devotional ministry. In retirement he stretched his wings a bit further. In 1972 he and Chris, with Alf and Margaret Cordiner of Aberdeen, spent two months in the Faroe Islands where he ministered in most of the assemblies. In 1974 they went to Southern Rhodesia, or Zimbabwe as it is now called, and South Africa doing the same. In 1976 South Africa was again visited.

John's written ministry wasn't large, probably because the man, being of a retiring disposition, never pushed himself forward. He contributed articles to "The Believers' Magazine," "The Witness" and "The Harvester", probably all of them solicited. He contributed articles to the symposia edited by J. B. Watson on "The Faith" and "The Church".

The writer recalls a few of John Rollo's addresses. How reverently he read Isa. 53 and drawing attention to the mentions of the word, "soul" in it he went on to stress that "the soul of

His suffering was the suffering of His soul." Speaking on the Lordship of Christ his three readings were from Acts 9, 10 and Phil. 3. In Acts 9 he illustrated from Saul's conversion story the confessing of Christ as Lord; from Acts 10 the contradiction of saying, as Peter did in v. 10, "Not so, Lord." Finally in Phil. 3:8 he made much of "the surpassing excellence of the knowledge of Christ Jesus as Lord."

John Rollo's deathbed was as lovely as his life. His final meditations were in John's Gospel. Said he, "I'm finding great joy in reading, and re-reading, in thinking and rethinking, on some of the words of frequent occurrence associated with the seven 'I Am's and the seven signs. A fortnight or so later he was gone, last words from a weary hospital ward being, "We're holding on to God".

JOHN RUDDOCK
(1897–1988)

JOHN RUDDOCK

John Ruddock was an Irishman, born in Growell in 1897. Although John's father was an evangelist he was twenty one before he was saved. Almost immediately he joined Ernest Wilson of the same assembly in tract distribution and open air work.

Owing to his father's ill health the family emigrated to the U.S., settling in Los Angeles where John continued his work for the Lord commencing a work among Mexicans which eventually led to an assembly being formed. John would have gone to Mexico as a missionary but it had been closed to such since about 1912. However he married Janet Nettie Baird who emigrated from Saltcoats in Ayrshire. They were commended from the Jefferson Gospel Hall to the Lord's work in Guatemala. First they worked in Quetatzaltenango and then in San Felipe. In 1931 they were commended from assemblies in Los Angeles to Honduras, where there was only one missionary couple, Alfred and Mrs. Hockings, working in the poorest and most backward of Central American Republics.

At first they worked with the Hockings for a year before moving to Trujillo where they worked among Carib Indians. Opposition was bitter but after four years they began to reap and an assembly was formed. Their final move was to Tela which was their base for the next thirty six years. In the earlier years travel was difficult but not impossible, so that by train, or on foot, or on mule back they travelled far and wide spreading the gospel. Frequent attacks of malaria did not deter them. John Ruddock preached the gospel, discipled converts, taught from house to house, built meeting halls, saw assemblies formed. From only one when they first went to Honduras, there are two hundred today, and they played a large part in planting them, and were still able to visit neighbouring countries, in company with others, like

Costa Rica and Nicaragua with the gospel.

The care of the elderly has not been a high priority in society, and not even among Christians. John Ruddock designed an Eventide Home in Tela and did much of the work himself. The Mayor of Tela spoke about it in these terms: "Speaking about the many works which have been accomplished the most extraordinary is the Old People's Home. Those who are fortunate enough to live in this home live a life of leisure and comfort, Everything is provided, shelter, food, clothing and medical attention. It is the work of a married couple, John and Nettie Ruddock. They did a good work in Trujillo, they then settled in Tela. I want to take this opportunity of advising the people of Tela about this work. If there is anything that should be recognised in Tela, it is that this work, in truth, is a wonderful asset to the city." As in the Dominican Republic a work that began in the face of stiff opposition from Roman Catholic priests, etc., came to be respected.

The Ruddocks retired to the Western Assemblies Home in California in 1978 but their work goes on. Quite recently Sam Hanlon has been able to complete an extension to the Home in Tela and it has been called after the Ruddocks, being opened by a member of their family. Their work continued in other ways. Real missionaries do not retire. They collected Spanish texts, affixed them to magazine-sized coloured pictures, and sent them, more than five hundred a month to Costa Rica, Guatemala, El Salvador, and Honduras as Sunday School prizes and as awards for work among adults.

As if that was not enough when he obtained a book on the History of the Ruddock clan, giving names and addresses of such all over the world, he wrote to them all giving his own life story and including the story of God's way of salvation. A few turned out to be believers, but he tried to maintain contact with all who responded.

Saved at twenty one he died at ninety one with a life packed full for God behind him. Less than a week before his homecall "Missions" magazine received one of his poems from him.

> "Hark the call from dark Honduras,
> Sounding through the air,
> Telling Christians in the homelands
> Of the need out there.

There the fields are ripe to harvest,
All of silver spray
Where, oh where then are the workers,
Toiling through the day?

The subtle enemy is busy,
Gathering in his share.
All around us are his agents,
Working everywhere.

Listen to the people crying
For the Gospel book
That they too may read the story,
Only found within that book.

Yes, they want to hear of Jesus,
And his wondrous love to man,
How He came to seek and save them,
Suffering on the cross of shame.

Some of us have gone to tell them
Of salvation's gracious plan
They've responded, hearts o'erflowing,
To the message of God's plan.

Now there's more who want to hear it,
But to them we cannot go.
Old age is now upon us,
Leaving us too weak to go.

You, my brother and my sister,
Young in body, sound in mind,
Why can't you go down and tell them,
The sweetest story ever found?

Remember sacrifices you'll have to make,
But you'll say it's worth it
When you see the people smile,
And hear the master say,
'Well done.' "

RALPH SHALLIS

Ralph Shallis was the son of missionaries. His father and mother, Mr. and Mrs. A. J. Shallis had served the Lord in Venezuela from 1904–1909, before transferring to Spain where they served the Lord in the Benevente Castrogonzalo area. Their son, Ralph, the subject of this article, said that he was brought up in the semi-desert plateau of Old Castile and learned to think in two languages. His later education was received in England where, to use his own words, he "encountered God" when he was eighteen years of age.

He taught languages and literature in several European countries, but at twenty-three he was still very dissatisfied with his life. The next three years, while working in the Swiss Alps, his life took on a different meaning. He read about Hudson Taylor, George Muller, John Bunyan, David Brainerd, C. T. Studd, Sadhu Sundar Singh, John Wesley, etc. They were all men of prayer. However the next five or six years of his life were devoured by World War Two, when as a conscript soldier he served in Africa, Asia and Europe. His wartime experiences deepened his spiritual life.

He gave one tenth of each day to reading and prayer. He divided the tenth into three spells of each with intervals. He learned not only to speak to God but also to let God speak to him. After the War he resumed his teaching career, in Portugal this time, settling down with his wife, Rangeley, whom he scarcely knew, although married for four years, because he had been away on active service for so long.

The next milestone in his spiritual career came when he was thirty seven years of age. It was then that he gave his all to Christ for service. So in 1949 he, with his wife and young family, settled in Muslim Algeria to proclaim the gospel. He identified with a little assembly at Hussein Day where he saw a remarkable work done. He himself wrote that he was overwhelmed and exhausted by the numbers of young men, etc., who came to Christ. Unfortunately the Algerian War broke out and Ralph had to come to England in 1957. While that phase of the work ended many Algerian Christians moved to France, including a number of those young men who went into full-time service for the Lord in France.

Ralph had now to concentrate his work on France. But the Spirit drove him all over France, and to nearly every European country, and beyond. "In the streets and universities, lecturing and by colportage, through sleepless nights and endless personal discussions, he faced up to the anguish of a generation no longer satisfied." His particular burden was for the young people of France and he settled in Grenoble.

But Ralph Shallis didn't only evangelise; he also wrote. He had as many as four titles together in the stocks at the same time. His book, "From Now On" was translated into English. He laughed at the idea of his books being translated into English considering that that was one of his native languages, but then he wanted it to serve and influence the people he was working among first. After all there is far more evangelical literature in English than in French. Most of the biographical material in this article is taken from that challenging book.

More than most Ralph's lifestory is dominated by clearly-defined landmarks or dates. In 1976 it was discovered that he had a severe form of leukaemia which certainly required a very different lifestyle from his former one. His burden for young folk was the same but he would have to write for them now rather than speak to them. His service for the Lord was as feverish as before. He must get those titles which he had in mind completed before he was called to higher service. He was able to keep on working until two days before his homecall, praising the Lord until the last. "Echoes of Service" wrote, "France has lost a unique, spiritual giant". He didn't pay many visits home, but where was home for Ralph? All who met him when he did come home could only describe him as "a holy man of God". If you didn't meet him, like the writer, sample the man from his writings.

WHEN MY HEART CRIES OUT

Just before the Second World War God gave me an experience of Himself that changed my whole concept of life. Then came the appalling folly and suffering of the War. God first opened my eyes to the vision of Himself; then He gave me a vision of the nations enmeshed in a web of hell. What could I do after that but give the rest of my life to making Christ known to men?

So at the young and rather foolish age of thirty five I began to tell my fellow-Christians that we must give priority to world evangelism. I insisted that, if we repented and obeyed God, we could see the greatest harvest of souls ever known; but that if we did not rise to the occasion we were in for the greatest persecution of all time. I think few understood; but for me it was a case of life and death.

So then, instead of telling the church what she ought to do, God told me to go and do it myself. This meant going and preaching where Christ is not known, and depending, as Christ taught His apostles, on God alone, even for money, food and clothing—for me, for my wife and my children.

It was tough. Most of all for my wife. Satan knows that the surest way to hit a man is through the woman. I learned a lot about his objectives and methods through that experience. But it is a fact that God brought us through those early years, sorely battered, but not so battered as our brothers in Siberian concentration camps. And He saved souls where men told us we could not expect God to work. He made them into men of God who have evangelised far more souls than we have. For me this was God's signature on His Word.

And now, years afterwards, I find myself again faced with the same question I started with: Will God revive the church? God has shown me, over and over again, that He will honour His Word and that His Spirit will act if He finds real faith in Christ— anywhere, to the point of utter obedience.

I have discovered that two or three believers integrated into Christ, welded into total spiritual cohesion with the one objective of doing God's will—and that is the evangelising of the nations— can take hold of God for the impossible. God can do more through such a tiny nucleus than through dozens of "ordinary" churches. Because the people who get converted are themselves grafted into the body of Christ on the highest spiritual level. From the day of their new birth they accept the apostolic vision. They learn to pray spontaneously, anywhere, at any time, however simply. They are not afraid to give God a good portion of their time each day. They learn to devour the New Testament, and then the whole Bible. They discover the miracle of true fellowship from the start. And they learn to take a clear stand for Christ and to do a real job of work for Him. What other kind of Christianity can kindle revival? What other kind can face the present world forces head on and win through—even if it costs fire, and blood, and tears, and everything else? What other kind can expect to survive *and grow* in the face of total persecution?

What alarms me today far more than the world tensions at explosion-point, than the countries that are more and more closing their doors to Christ, more even than the unforgivable moral cesspit of our Western society, is the seeming impotence of the church as a whole, the apathy, the disobedience and the inexplicable ignorance of the Scriptures and therefore of God Himself among the people of God. There are marvellous exceptions, thank God. But how can the judgement of God wait if we are no longer the light of the world? Brother, sister let us get rid of everything that prevents the Spirit of God from taking our faith seriously.

JESUS CHRIST WILL HAVE THE LAST
WORD, SPEAK, LORD!

Ralph Shallis

Ralph's advice to young Christians: "Read the whole Bible through every year. Begin with the New Testament. Read both concurrently. Read consecutively. Take notes under subjects.

G

JAMES M. S. TAIT
(1903–1980)

JAMES M. S. TAIT

Mr. James M. S. Tait was born in the small crofting community of Clousta, Shetland in 1903. As a young lad he had a great thirst for knowledge, but educational opportunities were few in those days. He was obliged to leave school at fourteen years of age in order to augment the family income. Books held a fascination for him and it was through reading "The Traveller's Guide" as a teenager that he was converted. That book was bought at the door from a travelling colporteur. The price was 6d, which neither James nor his mother possessed at the time, so sister Elsie came to the rescue, and James got saved.

It seemed clear to him at the time that he should follow a seafaring career like many of his contemporaries, but although he went to Leith to join a ship he was unsuccessful and returned to Shetland to take up work as a roadman. His sister brought him to a meeting in Ebenezer Hall, Lerwick. It was a baptismal service and he was greatly impressed by the straightforward interpretation of the scriptures and the way the New Testament was brought to life and given fresh meaning. It left an indelible impression and soon he was baptised and joined the fellowship.

Another event changed the course of his life about this time. While having breakfast in a hut with some other workmen, someone put a stick of gelignite beside a stove to dry. There was a violent explosion which blew the hut and the stove into fragments, and James Tait received serious leg injuries which caused him to walk with a slight limp ever afterwards. While recovering in hospital he realised he would have to change his occupation and so prepared himself for an office job. He obtained work as a clerk to a local solicitor, who soon saw his capabilities and encouraged him to take up the legal profession as a career.

In his spare time Mr. Tait educated himself by taking correspondence courses and attending night school. He distinguished himself as a law student at Edinburgh University and on qualifying as a solicitor in 1935, he returned to Lerwick and shortly afterwards acquired his former employer's business, which he developed into the largest law practice in Shetland.

His ability as a preacher and expositor was soon recognised by the assembly at Ebenezer Hall, Lerwick. Since his first introduction to the assembly he saw the value of expository preaching, and prepared himself by learning New Testament Greek and studying the scriptures extensively. He developed the gift of saying much in few words, with apt topical illustrations. His love of nature and the wonders of creation were frequently present in his messages. His mastery of the English language, profound knowledge of the scriptures, and poetic turn of mind ensured the rapt attention of his hearers, and this combined with a deep spiritual insight and true humility, often left a lasting impression.

He frequently gave consecutive Bible teaching in Ebenezer Hall, Lerwick such as the signs in John's Gospel, the messages to the Seven Churches, or the systematic exposition of an Old Testament Book or New Testament epistle. The typical and the mystical were present but he was never guilty of "balancing a pyramid on its apex" to use his own words. Not only was he an able speaker but he was also an attentive listener, and had the ability to extract spiritual profit from the efforts of all others. The conversational Bible reading gave him an opportunity to develop and expand the thoughts of others and he could also with grace and skill turn an unprofitable discussion into a deeply spiritual lesson.

Mr. Tait had a keen sense of humour and was excellent company on any occasion. His gracious manner made him an ideal door-keeper, and he delighted to hand out the hymnbooks with a cheery welcome to the folk as they arrived for a meeting.

It is unfortunate that James Tait was not known to a wider audience outside the Shetland Islands as he could certainly have shared a platform with some of the best known conference speakers, but because of his retiring disposition it is doubtful if he would have accepted such an invitation. He has not left much written ministry apart from a few magazine articles, but some indication of his facility of expression and deep spirituality will be readily appreciated on perusing his book of poems, "Bells and Pomegranates" published in 1946. It was reprinted in an enlarged edition in 1985 to mark the centenary of Ebenezer Hall and included most of his previously unpublished poems.

Needless to say, the work of the Lord in Shetland has been greatly furthered by the godly example and teaching of James Tait and other likeminded servants of God. The assembly at Ebenezer Hall, Lerwick, in particular, was built up spiritually and numerically.

George Peterson

James Tait was no amateur poet. Some half dozen of his poems are based on the tabernacle and related subjects. They showed how keen an insight he had into the spiritual meaning of those difficult parts of the Bible. We append a splendid example taken from "Bells and Pomegranates" which is still available, as it was reprinted.

THE BURDEN AND THE SONG

"The Service of the burden," (Num. 4:47)
"The Service of song." (1 Chron. 6:31)

All through the desert's sultry day
A weary load to carry;
Who envied then the toilsome way
Of Kohath and Merari?

Now priest and ark alike find rest
Where God His temple raises;
And they who served with burdens pressed,
Now only serve with praises.

How perfect are the ways of God!
How just His compensation!
How long the path they humbly trod;
How high their exaltation.

No needless load on thee He'll lay,
No unrequited sorrow,
The burden-bearer of today,
Is the singer of tomorrow.

F. A. TATFORD
(1901–1986)

F. A. TATFORD

Fred Tatford was born into a Christian home in Southsea, Hants, on February 22, 1901 where love was more readily available than luxury. If he was not brought up in the lap of luxury he was brought up under Christian principles. As early as his school days he was interested in writing and editing, for he produced a hand-written magazine. Lack of resources prevented him going to university although his ability was undoubted. Herbert Lockyer said about him that he could have made a fortune for himself if he had been utterly devoted to business interests.

One Sunday in December, 1915, when Fred was nearly fifteen years of age he was saved. Shortly afterwards he was baptised at a service attended by many of his school friends. He was brought up in an assembly, but had to leave home just after he became seventeen and go into lodgings, since he had received his first appointment in the Civil Service. He spent much of his free time in his local assembly, while at work he earned a reputation as a "Bible puncher". His next digs brought him to Central Hall, Wimbledon, where the leading brother was Theo Churchill, a relative of Sir Winston. It was here that Fred became a real Bible student. It was here too that he met his wife, Miss Grace Vince. He started preaching when he was nineteen and in his excitement read the wrong passage.

He early showed an interest in prophecy attending a meeting of the Advent Testimony and Preparation Movement in 1917, where he heard Walter Scott, then ninety three years of age speaking on the Second Coming. Thereafter he bought Walter Scott's book on Revelation and read every book by him on which he could lay hands. He would have liked to have become a missionary and consulted W. E. Vine about it, receiving the advice to study. He kept up an enormous interest in missionary matters but later asked the question, "Why give up a secular job to serve the Lord when you can preach with your life on the job?" He did and became Secretary of the Civil Service Christian Union for the years 1923–1927.

All the time his ability was growing along with his willingness to serve the Lord. The inter-war years were the great years for Christian rallies, principally for young people on Saturday nights, and Fred touched such almost every weekend in the winter season so much so that there were few towns in the U.K. in which he has not preached. He also helped to convene such rallies at Wembley and Wallington. At home he conducted a Young Men's Class on Friday evenings from 1933–1936, and from 1932–1939 organised a Young People's Holiday Conference.

Fred's first post in the Civil Service was in the Board of Education. After passing some Civil Service exams he moved to Inland Revenue. Inland Revenue was evacuated to North Wales for the duration of World War Two and Fred, not wanting to go, moved into the Ministry of Supply in 1940, becoming in time Deputy Assistant Director of Contracts. He later joined the Department of Atomic Energy as Director of Contracts. Becoming an expert on Contract Law he wrote articles on it for Chamber's Encyclopaedia.

It was in 1933 that Fred became editor of "The Harvester". He had been writing on spiritual matters for some time. Articles by him were appearing in the "Believers' Magazine" in 1931. In fact his first article had appeared in "Marching Orders" in 1923. His first book, entitled "Person and Work of the Devil" was published in 1928 in the post-war period. He obtained two Doctorates of Divinity, one Ph.D and a LL.D.—was Associate Editor of the "Prophetic Digest" of America, and declined an invitation to be editor of the "Moody Monthly" in 1948, which would have required a move to the U.S.A.

Fred Tatford's interest in things Christian was wide. He edited the "Prophetic Witness" for twenty four years. He was on the Council of the Arabic Literature Mission, of the International Jews Society, of the Far East Broadcasting Association, of the Nile Mission Press, the Child Evangelism Fellowship. He was Vice-President of Christian Friends of Israel, Christian Colportage Association, Evolution Protest Movement, Victory

Tract Club, etc.

A heart condition caused him to slow down a bit in 1971 a few years after his retirement. In spite of all his public service Fred Tatford was not an extrovert. He was shy, sensitive and caring. When Grace took ill he gladly nursed her for six months, laying aside his other responsibilities to do so. After she was called home he lived in a single room in an Eastbourne hotel to which town and assembly he had moved in 1965. He was content in those restricted quarters until he met Sylvia whom he married in 1983.

Dr. Tatford had a heart for the world. He never became a missionary but he had a wide missionary interest. When Civil Service duties took him overseas he looked up assemblies and missionaries wherever he went. He visited Belgium, Italy, Poland, Romania about which he could tell the story of being followed by the Secret Police, Czechoslovakia, Greece, Germany, Denmark, Yugoslavia, Austria, the Faroes, Zimbabwe, South Africa, Bermuda, Bahamas, Singapore, Malaysia, Hong Kong, etc. He was therefore freely consulted by the editors of "Echoes of Service" about missionary matters. His favourite country was France where his only son has been a missionary for many years, and almost every assembly in France has had a visit from Fred Tatford. The last country he visited was Spain just a short time before his homecall.

When "Echoes of Service" was having its centenary celebrated Fred played a large part in the production of the centenary volume, "Turning the World Upside Down." From the barebones of that volume Dr. Tatford conceived the idea of producing a definitive history of that great missionary movement and undertook the task, when he was eighty, of writing it in ten volumes. As with all of his books they were done in handwriting. Volumes 1-9 had been published and he read the proofs of Vol. 10 when the Lord called him home, his work done.

In a very real sense of Fred Tatford it could be said that he being dead yet speaketh. He lives on, not only in those missionary books, but also in about a hundred others. His first major work, "Prophecy's Last Word" was written in an air raid shelter during World War Two. Another series written in retirement and entitled "The 20th Century series", was devoted to the minor prophets, ten in all. His books were translated into

French, German, Serbo-Croatian, Faroese, Korean, etc. And as if that was not enough his library was transported to France to the L'Eau Vive Centre, the creation of his son Dr. Briand Tatford. It was unveiled by his widow and called the Maranatha Library.

Fred's utter devotion to the pre-millennialist interpretation of prophecy, advanced in the "Harvester" as long as he was editor, is illustrated in the following quotations taken from his biography, written by John McNicol, and entitled "20th Century Prophet".

"What nonsense to say that only those who are watching and waiting will be caught up to meet the Lord in the air. I was not saved on the basis of my morality or good life. I was saved by the grace of God revealed at Calvary. I have not kept myself once by my own ability. I have been kept by the power of God. I shall not be caught up to meet the Lord in the air because I was vigilantly watching for him. I shall go because I belong to him. It all depends on him not me."

"Some Christians believe that at least part of the Church will pass through the Great Tribulation. Fancy talking about the blessed hope of the tribulation. They can have my share of that free and for nothing."

And after a life of such devotion it is worth pondering these. "If you are not prepared to accept Christ as Lord do not insult him by calling him your Saviour."

"How often our awareness of our own ability hinders the work of God. If we were totally surrendered to the control of the Holy Spirit and filled by his mighty power, what God could do is beyond our imagination."

Mr. & Mrs. FRED WHITMORE
(1903–1980)

FRED WHITMORE

Fred Whitmore was born into a Christian family in Birmingham in 1903. When he was just ten he was led to the Lord Jesus by his father in his own kitchen. Even his teenage days saw him pretty well committed to the Lord's service. At thirteen he was given a Sunday School class in the same Gospel Hall. An assembly outreach was commenced in a school near Aston Villa football ground, called the Witton Mission, and for a number of years young Fred was the leader of this. Many were saved as a result. He was also much involved in the assembly's open air effort when they preached on dark nights under the light of an acetylene lamp on a pole.

But larger fields were calling young Fred and at the early age of twenty one he was commended to full-time service. At first he served the Lord with Counties Evangelistic Work, in Essex possibly, but he was in Bedfordshire in 1925. It was 1925 when he first met a Devon man, Harold German at St. Albans and they obviously felt that they could work well together.

While Harold German was praying for a partner to work with him in Yorkshire Fred wrote to say that he would be happy to join him, which he did in Ossett in 1926. The year of the General Strike was a wonderful year weather-wise and as far as Ossett and the Yorkshire Tent was concerned a wonderful year spiritually. Souls were saved every night. On the last Saturday of the campaign a baptismal service was held in Kennington Hall, Bradford, two special carriages being booked on a train and these were packed to capacity. Altogether thirty five were baptised that night. The next morning the new believers broke bread in the tent and the Ossett assembly commenced.

In 1927 the tent was pitched in Skelmanthorpe and Emley. On the last night at Emley a pit was dug outside the tent and lined with canvas. A hosepipe was borrowed and the pit filled with water. Fifty newly-saved people were baptised that evening. The next morning they met at Skelmanthorpe and the assembly continues till this day. In 1929 at Morley and Ravensthorpe there was again much blessing. At the end of the summer the two evangelists bought a Ford motor caravan with which to carry on open air work.

Naturally the two young men were jubilant at the way in which the Lord was blessing them and back to Devon they went to tell their story. Mr. German, senior, obviously thought they needed to be taken down a peg, so he told them that as a farmer he was always very particular about who should do the sowing, but that when it came to harvesting he went into the village and called in the help of any Tom, Dick and Harry.

Following this the two evangelists took their first trip into Scotland. They preached in many towns and villages travelling as far north as Inverurie in Aberdeenshire. They experienced blessing there and were invited back the next year for a Gospel campaign. It was here that both found their partners, Fred marrying in the early part of 1932 and Harold in December. Harold stayed on in Aberdeenshire for the rest of his life, while the Whitmores returned to Yorkshire. Some two years later Fred and Dorothy moved across the Pennines into Lancashire, where he was to spend the rest of his life.

Fred and Dorothy first came to Ayrshire in 1941. Dorothy was always one of the team. They had no family so that she was always free to accompany him. She played the organ, joined in the visitation and counselling, and greatly helped in the children's meetings. The old Ayrshire Gospel Tent was done. His first effort at Prestwick Toll was occupied patching it, since it was impossible to replace it during the War. Fred came to the county in 1941 and brought his own tent. This he did for the next three seasons after which he sold it to the Ayrshire brethren. During those four years he conducted campaigns in seven or eight places, saw results and made lasting friends. He felt that the Prestwick Toll effort was a total failure but on the same night many years later two ladies told him of their conversion during that time and one of them was then a missionary in the Belgian Congo, Rae Masterton, first of Renfrew and later of New Zealand.

Fred was one of the founders of the Lancashire Gospel Tent.

He was so much identified with it that many people called it Mr. Whitmore's tent. He worked it for twenty years, conducting twenty four campaigns of six weeks each. In several places, including Wythenshawe in Manchester, and Chorley new assemblies were established following the meetings. He liked to finish off campaigns with a few nights of ministry for young converts, dealing with subjects like baptism, fellowship, etc. He liked to conduct children's meetings as part of those campaigns, and the writer confesses that his biggest surprise with Fred Whitmore was his skill in attracting youngsters to his meetings, and in holding their attention while they were there. He loved to take a photo of those attending and used that promise as a means of keeping them coming for the appropriate unknown night, while providing himself with a permanent visual reminder of each campaign.

The Whitmores also ventured into foreign parts—the West Indies, Canada and the U.S.A. While in the West Indies he contributed articles to "The Carribbean Courier" out of which came his pamphlet on the Feasts of Jehovah.

Dorothy's homecall came suddenly and unexpectedly and it was as if the light of Fred's life had gone out. Eventually Miss Peggy Jenkins gave up her employment and invited him to her home where she cared for him for the last five years of his life. The Whitmores had stayed in her parents' home in Golborne for ten weeks when they had the Lancashire Tent in Golborne and the friendship lasted. She described the effort. "At that time the assembly was very small ... There had never been anything like it in the village. Souls were saved and several people restored. Soon after a new hall was built. Mr. Whitmore came very frequently for Gospel and ministry meetings over the years and was a tremendous help." Her expression of appreciation for most of the rest of his life was to nurse him in his declining days.

Fred's balanced outlook was evidenced in the Friday night Bible study for young Christians that he and the late E. Ogden commenced for young Christians in the county, and these continue still under the leadership of Harold Cooper and Tony Renshaw. They believed that suitable Bible studies were necessary for new converts.

HAROLD WILDISH
(1903–1982)

HAROLD WILDISH

Harold Wildish grew up in the West Country, attending Clarence School in Weston-Super-Mare. Quite a number of his school-mates came from assembly homes and as many as forty would march along on Sunday mornings to the Breaking of Bread service at Waterloo Road. One of the senior boys and young Harold's hero, was Crawford Tilsley, called after his uncle, Dan Crawford, and eventually himself a missionary in India for forty six years.

It was at a Gospel Meeting addressed by the Welsh evangelist, Garnet Thomas, that Harold was saved when he was just twelve and a half. At seventy one he was still praising God for a Christian home, a Christian school and the assembly.

Harold's parents moved to Westcliff-on-Sea in Essex in 1918 and it was here that he was baptised in 1920 and received into fellowship. His first service for the Lord was with a boy's class in Sunday School, and in the open air meetings in Westcliff High Street and Sea Front, as well as in the Essex villages.

His first job was in London in the Irish linen trade and at a missionary meeting in London the Lord made it clear to him that he was to serve overseas. He resigned his job and joined home evangelists for a year or two learning as he went. In particular he owed much to Sam Glen, a Scotsman working in Essex, and James Hodson, a Yorkshire man working in the West Country. From them he learned how to approach, interest and hold a crowd with a gospel message. He considered that their lives of faith, love for souls and Bible teaching were the best training he could have had for Gospel preaching and assembly planting in South America and in the West Indies where the Lord led him.

In 1925 he left Liverpool for Georgetown, British Guiana where the work was already nearly one hundred years old. He met veteran missionaries, Thomas Wales, Wilson Nicholas, George Baverstock and Henry Hale and learned much in the fifteen months he spent there. He described it as a Gospel preachers' paradise—open airs everywhere, meeting rooms, markets, schools and prisons, in towns along the coast, up the rivers and into the forests. Over eight hundred broke bread in the Camp Street meeting room, there were thirty six assemblies, and two outreaches among the Arawak Indians. Harold developed an interest in the savage tribes of the Amazon and left Guiana, with the approval of his brethren, for Brazil. On his way he went through French Guiana and made the need known.

Harold arrived at Manaos, 1,000 miles up the Amazon. Christian friends accompanied Harold in his search for Indians and contact was made through gifts, sitting round camp fires, sharing their roasted food and learning words from their language. Philip Tate joined Harold in 1928 and they too used a launch to sell Bibles at settlements up the Perus River where at Cobija in North Bolivia they sold Bibles in the morning which were confiscated and burned in the afternoon by the priest. That work subsequently prospered under Mr. and Mrs. Ned Meharg. Returning to Manaus, where John and Claudete Axford now work, Harold went down with malignant malaria. Doctor said, "Either leave the country or stay under the ground." Disappointed, Harold had to leave Brazil for the West Indies. He wrote a book on his experiences, entitled, "Among the Savage Indians of the Amazon," published by Pickering and Inglis. H. P. Barker and Albert Widdison were conducting an evangelistic tour of the Islands and invited Harold to join them. This increased Harold's experience and his health greatly improved. Many professed to be saved and Harold had the joy of returning to Guiana along with them. A further six months were spent at home where he married Miss Marion Arrol in 1928. (She was one of a marvellous group of Christian nurses who trained together in London becoming Mrs. Wildish of the West Indies, Mrs. Shniednook of Poland, and Mrs. Morse of Zambia, who later married Phil Simmons of "Echoes").

Once again Harold, accompanied by his wife, set out for the Amazon, but an urgent call came to relieve sick workers in Guiana so they spent two years there, but malaria struck again so that they had to make the West Indies their permanent sphere of service from 1932 onwards.

The writer's personal recollection is of hearing Harold Wildish during his next furlough and although just a young boy and unsaved the memory remains. He was such a powerful personality that I still recall him speaking on the title of God, "El Shaddai". Another person, who heard him speaking to children about the Flood, claimed that he could almost see it happening because it was so vividly described.

He returned to Jamaica in 1936 accompanied by Edwin Willy, a Cardiff businessman, who shared many gospel campaigns with him. Using a tent seating eight hundred it was usual for it to be full with hundreds standing inside and out. Some missions lasted three or four months, and counsellors could be pointing folk to the Saviour while others were instructing those newly saved. The Kingston assembly grew to eight hundred while the Assembly Hall grew to six hundred. Five hundred professed at another campaign in another area.

The war years were spent at home and Harold engaged with others in work among the forces, returning to Jamaica in a banana boat.

Edwin Willy accompanied him on this trip and a campaign in another part of Kingston resulted in the Galilee assembly being formed. On a Good Friday seventy eight converts were baptised in the sea. 1947 saw the tent in another area and another assembly was formed. In 1948 Olivet assembly grew to four hundred with 1,000 children in the Sunday School. In all, four new assemblies came into existence. One immigrant said, "They don't call us Christians in Jamaica, they call us Wildish-men."

A 1946 campaign in St. Kitts saw thirty added to an assembly. A memorable visit was made to Trinidad. Four times visits were made to Belize in support of Jamaican workers there. He made many visits to the Bahamas, one of them in 1938 with Edwin Willy when large numbers were saved. Harold Wildish conducted such gospel campaigns on the American mainland in Canada and the U.S.A., in Ecuador and Panama, in Singapore and New Zealand.

He wrote in 1981: "Many a time when facing a crowd of 2,000 listening to the gospel I have thought of the few dozen Redskins round the campfires in the Amazon who seemed so hard to reach, and wondered that the Lord had spared us and given us an easier job."

Increasingly his work turned to ministry grounding the young in the truth. He was content to stay in the little corner of the vineyard where the Lord had placed them.

DAVID WILLCOX
(1914–1988)

DAVID WILLCOX

David Willcox virtually spent all of his service for the Lord in two English counties, Dorset and Somerset. Growing up in the former he gave almost a quarter of a century to evangelising it while "tent-making" or to be accurate shoemaking. The next quarter of a century was given full-time, in the fullest sense of the word, to Somerset.

David Stanley Willcox was born in a caravan situated in an orchard in Stalbridge, Dorset in 1914. His father too was an evangelist and the caravan was probably of his own construction, for he was an inventor in his own right. He buit several caravans in which he travelled around until the birth of his third child when they settled in Shaftesbury, Dorset where he developed a shoe repair business.

Young David left school at sixteen years of age and went to work with his father in the shoemaker's shop. At the same age he conducted his first service and preached his first sermon. Preparing for this he committed his whole life to serving the Lord. At eighteen years of age he commenced scripture text banner work and he and others went to all the fairs and carnivals around with tracts and banners. They were often taunted and had missiles like tomatoes and eggs thrown at them. Later on they extended this kind of activity to race courses as well.

When National Service claimed David during the Second World War he claimed exemption as a Conscientious Objector, which exemption was allowed, as his father's business included the repair of army boots and shoes. He married Eileen Dawin in 1950, the sister of his banner-carrying companions. They continued to live in Shaftesbury, fellowshipping in Shillingstone Gospel Hall, working at shoe repairing, but engaging in a lot of evangelistic work in surrounding villages. They distributed tracts and held gospel meetings in hired village halls and borrowed gospel halls.

His brother-in-law joined the shoe business in 1960 while David increasingly helped the Counties Evangelistic Worker in Dorset, Nelson Walker, doing practically all of the children's work. Their routine became rising at 5 a.m. and working at shoe repairing until noon, and then travelling to join the Walkers wherever they were missioning in Dorset.

Such activity could only lead to full-time service and David's exercise was to become an evangelist in Somerset, the neighbouring county. In 1963 he was accepted by Counties as their evangelist for Somerset, and was commended to the work by the Shillingstone assembly. Two years later they moved to a rented house in Glastonbury.

David had a great love for the small assemblies of Somerset. He would hold children's missions and try to build up those little companies of the Lord's people. He would hire village halls and conduct missions in them. In the summer months he would erect his tent and conduct three to five missions. The spring and autumn would see him engaged in another three, four or five missions. He learned the art of tent erection, dismantling, etc., during the three years he had worked with Nelson Walker and became quite an expert at it.

In 1967 he commenced beach missions, first in Weston-super-Mare for four years, and then each year for the rest of his life at Blue Anchor and Minehead. The Blue Anchor beach was the venue for the morning meeting, while the afternoon one was held at Minehead. In 1987 Dunster Beach was added as well.

Eileen was called home suddenly in 1973. She had always been a keen partner in his work. In 1974 David married Elsie, District Nurse in Glastonbury. Both worked wholeheartedly with their husband to further the gospel of the Lord Jesus. The next year an annual camp was commenced to teach Christian young people more of the Scriptures, especially with the view of encouraging them to throw in their lot with their local assembly and to grow in divine things. The first camp was attended by thirty youngsters but it grew to one hundred and eighty, so two camps had to be run. An Easter weekend was commenced for the same purpose and this was extended to a whole week at the young people's request. Here again David gave more assembly teaching and many were baptised as a result and came into fellowship.

In 1976 David commenced a witness at the Bath and West Agricultural Show. A good artist he designed the exhibit himself. One of his last outings was to see to the site for the 1989 Show which he was not to attend in person. That show attracts 150,000 people every year.

"Evangelism Today" carried an article about David's summer work. It said, "One of the busiest 'holiday' evangelists has been David Willcox. I called on him at Watchet on the North Somerset coast. His two hundred seater tent was pitched on a council housing estate, but when I arrived he was away with his team of six youngsters, conducting an open-air witness in Minehead. For the whole of August his daily timetable consists of a morning Beach service for children at Blue Anchor Caravan site, an afternoon of witness at one of the holiday resorts, a children's meeting in the Tent at Watchet, and an evening activity for adults or young people in the big tent. He certainly keeps his team busy. Still, as he says, 'We're preaching to literally thousands of holidaymakers like this.'"

David's own report said that regular numbers at Blue Anchor ranged from 70–100 with good numbers of adults listening. During the afternoons the team reached thirty places and held over sixty open-air meetings, distributing hundreds of gospel leaflets.

Getting older David never let up. He was constantly looking for new avenues of service. In 1987 he commenced a Postal Bible Sunday School which is still thriving with over sixty youngsters and two or three adults studying the courses. Philip Dalling, conducting his funeral service, said that while David had given up text-carrying he had taken to wearing a conspicuous lapel badge declaring, "Jesus Saves." His funeral took place in December, 1988 and Philip remarked that had he been alive he would likely have been among the Christmas shopping crowds somewhere in Somerset witnessing for his Lord.

It was during the summer of 1986 that David began to have pain in his leg. Treatment did not succeed, but the Lord's servant carried on. Radiotherapy had no effect, but David was still serving his Lord until within a month of his homecall. His long-standing exercise was that people of all ages should be taught the Word of God.

Many look back on David as their spiritual father, a man who cared a great deal about their growth and establishment in Christ. Others have learned the thrust of evangelism as they shared events alongside this hardworking man.

R. J. WRIGHT
(1906–1988)

R. J. WRIGHT

Bobby Wright was the son of an Irish evangelist. He was saved at the age of eleven, and baptised four years later in a quarry hole whose ice covering had to be broken before the baptism could take place. He described his spiritual progress as slow, but he helped to organise open air meetings and to hold Sunday School classes for one hundred and fifty children in a corrugated iron hut in Milltown, Dugannon.

"Echoes of Service" was always lying about the house and many missionaries stayed in the home so that young Bobby was conditioned to think about missionary work. The absence of three countries from "Echoes of Service" challenged him: Colombia with six million people, Dutch E. Indies with sixty five million and Japan with ninety million. So he settled for Japan, in which he decided to seek employment. Christian businessmen in London could give him opportunities in the Argentine, or in India, but not in Japan. He contacted C. B. K. Argall, a Cornish chemist working in Japan to offer his services. The reply was: "It would be cheaper ... to employ a white Russian chemist from Shanghai. However you may send me a cable address, just in case." Argall took ill and had to invite Bobby to join him, and to continue with him afterwards when he discovered how much more lucrative teaching English was than running a chemist's shop.

In 1931 Japan was thirty five days away from Ulster. Taking farewell with family Bobby had the assurance that he would see his father again, but not so his brother, on earth or in heaven. This truth brought his brother to the Saviour the night before Bobby left home. He arrived in Japan to discover that he was not the first assembly missionary as he had just been beaten to this honour by the Hays of Tyneside who came to Japan to learn Japanese before proceeding to Formosa. They formed the first assembly in Japan of two peopie, Bobby's arrival increasing their size by half.

But all of Bobby's contacts in the chemist's shop were English-speaking so his knowledge of Japanese was not being advanced, and he decided to move out of the Argall's home and employment. He moved to Tokyo 300 miles away to join a young Japanese believer who had visited him at intervals, cycling all the way and distributing tracts as he went. The two rented a disused coffee shop which they used as living quarters, and as a meeting place. It seated thirty six people and was used as a walk-in meeting place every night for six years, people coming and going throughout the evening with preachers rotating as well, the young Japanese brother and his doctor employer carrying the burden of the responsibility, while other new Japanese converts and Bobby helped out and he became more and more proficient in the language.

The Hays had started a witness in Kobe before going to Formosa. A newly-converted dentist with more zeal than knowledge was left in charge, and Bobby felt he was needed there. His new living accommodation was difficult, as was the work, and Bobby nearly had a break-down. He therefore decided to have a furlough but chose to have it by travelling over the land route of the Trans-Siberian Railway. After a year at home Bobby returned to Japan in 1938 and soon after was joined by John Hewitt who sold his farm in Ulster to join in the work.

World War Two was drawing nearer and in many ways Japan was following Hitler's example. Bowing to shrines implying the worship of the Emperor was deemed idol worship by Christians, and not bowing as subversive by Government. Tract work was banned and police activity stopped parents allowing children to attend Sunday School. In 1941 the first Christians were arrested and imprisoned, Bobby and John Hewitt among them. Both were advised to leave the country. Bobby was being evacuated to America, John to follow later, but he was detained, certified insane and held in captivity—a very real martyr for Christ's sake. Meantime Bobby's boat turned and headed back to Japan—because of Pearl Harbour when Japan entered the War. Again Bobby found himself interned and it was eight months before he was released to be returned to Britain.

Obviously return to Japan was impossible for Bobby while the

War continued, so he took a job. He also married, and influenced half a dozen people to set their minds on serving the Lord in Japan once the War was over. However it was 1948 before the Wrights succeeded in reaching the land of the Rising Sun. That land had the highest literacy rate in the world so that Christian literacy is an obvious way of reaching the people. So from the beginning Tom Hay and Bobby Wright engaged in literature work, laying the foundations of the Evangelical Publishing Depot which has circulated millions of gospel tracts. From tracts they went on to translate good gospel booklets and then Christian books.

It was after World War Two that Korea was opened to the gospel. Bobby Wright was anxious to send Christian literature into it. He got "The Reason Why" translated into that language and despatched to the country. Distributors there being on the point of returning to their homelands, Bobby paid a memorable visit to ensure that such work would continue.

His own experience in prison made Bobby Wright interested in Japanese prisons. Post-war Japan gave foreigners freedom such as they had never had before so that Bobby found it easy to gain admission. Soon a Bible Class was going in a very large prison and occasionally Bobby had the privilege of addressing the staff and prisoners, numbering 1,500 in the prison auditorium. And this was only one of the prisons to which Mr. Wright had access. Eileen too played a part in this kind of work as she visited a Girls' Reform School weekly. This work was extended even further when access was gained to the war criminal prison.

Bobby's partner in this last work was Conrad Baehr, an American who had evangelised in China. Forced to leave China he took a job, but the Pocket Testament League sent him to Japan to help meet General McArthur's request for a million gospels for that country. Conrad sought Bobby's help with regard to size, type, etc., and eventually five million pocket Testaments were distributed at rallies throughout the country. A notable convert was the Air Flight Commander who gave the order for bombing Pearl Harbour.

Unfortunately all of this personal involvement in Japanese evangelisation was brought to a halt by an injury to Bobby's back which resulted in months of agony and no successful treatment. He just had to return home, but the Japanese

Government decided to honour him for his prison work. At an elaborate ceremony the first foreigner to be so honoured was presented with an illuminated address and a silver memorial cup by the Minister of Justice. He was also given the opportunity of addressing all prisoners in Japan for ten minutes over the closed circuit prison T.V. service and did not miss the opportunity. He was stretchered on to the ship for the voyage home.

The family set up home in Carrickfergus where Bobby had bought property pre-war. He heard of a chemist's business for sale in Bangor, but in a street where there were four other such businesses. However he took it and although it was a struggle to begin with Bobby managed. His wife resumed teaching and ended as Deputy Headmistress of her school. Eventually Bobby moved into Belfast which saved a lot of travelling. Finally once the troubles had started, Bobby's premises were broken into so frequently that insurance companies would not cover them. This gave him the opportunity to get out and for the rest of his working life he was happy to act as locum in chemist's shops giving him an income without responsibility, and free time to engage in his first love—evangelism.

He began to visit terrorists in Long Kesh Camp and a small Bible class grew up. Several prisoners trusted the Saviour. Read this: "I first heard about Bobby in 1983, due to the lads round about me talking about him. My first meeting with him is one I'll never forget. I was going to speak to him about 'outside'. The conversation was about 'outside' alright—my soul outside of heaven. His manner of introducing himself was: 'I'm Bobby Wright—are you saved? Do you know where you're heading?' The lads called him 'our da'. He never gave up. In wind, rain or snow he was always up to see 'his wee apprentices.'"

He was able to revisit Japan in 1978. They spent seven weeks visiting the four main islands. It was V.I.P. treatment all the way. After all one fellow-missionary wrote, "Only the Lord knows what the work in Japan owes to Bobby's zeal, and leadership, and hard work. He had a direct influence on many of the things that happen here, but his indirect influence is beyond what any man could measure. Like many others I'm quite sure that I would never have been in Japan if it hadn't been for the way he made the country and its need known. Just about everybody in Japan has a story to tell about Bobby."

212

Although approaching eighty there was still something of the pioneer in Bobby. Near home, a few miles from Carrickfergus, there is a small seaside town of Whitehead. With a few others Bobby had a desire to raise a witness for Christ there. First he bought a corner site, and then a hut, already used as the first stage in the outreach that preceded three other assemblies. Then in 1985 George Bates came to preach, every home in the community having been visited and provided with a copy of "God's Way of Salvation." And so another assembly came into existence in Ulster. Bobby came the opening evening with a smile on his face and lines of suffering on his brow. His back pain was severe and he had to stop his prison visitation and his Wednesday Bible study for housewives. The end came on May 3, 1988 and his funeral was the first to be held in Whitehead Gospel Hall. To the end he was coaxing, persuading, shaming, convincing, leading or nudging individuals into the kingdom.

Bobby Wright was not only an energetic evangelist and constant prodder of believers and unbelievers alike, he was also a man who knew the reality of sacrificial stewardship. Not only did he urge people what to do, but he did it all himself. He was a channel in the Lord's hand of help to many. He transferred a quantity of shares in a trading company to a Missionary Service Organisation when most people would have been enjoying the dividends themselves or giving them to their family. There are also examples of gifts sent to him being passed on to others who surprised donors by acknowledging gifts sent to Bobby Wright.

He eventually had the joy of seeing a member of his family become a missionary. Even at her wedding he had urged the importance of serving the Lord abroad upon the young couple. He attended their Farewell Meeting in a crowded school hall in Paisley and he was so typical of himself. He addressed us thus, "I don't like you Scots. We have missionaries from England in Japan, and from Ireland, we have them from Canada and America, we have them from Australia and New Zealand, we even had them from Holland and from Germany, but we have none from Scotland." He never saw Marlyn and her husband Ian and grandchildren afterwards. They set out for Zaire and thirteen months later her dad went home to glory.

Bobby Wright was a character of the first order. He hated humbug and insincerity. He issued a Dictionary for young

Preachers at one stage in his life. It was satirical of course, a collection of "brethren" jargon such as so many of us fall into. "His self-supporting attitude laid a good foundation for Japanese assemblies to follow," said his obituary in "Echoes of Service" magazine. He was a man with a wonderful sense of humour, but above all with a deep love for the Lord whom he served for so many years."

His biography entitled "No Greater Joy" was written by a very Catholic lady, Bernie Reid, saved at that effort in the new Bethany Hall in Whitehead and fascinated by one of the most unusual characters Ulster has ever produced.

Bill Funston sums it all up with this tribute: "There is no man among those in assemblies who has made a greater impact on the world mission scene, for his vision was for the whole world, not just Japan. I remember hearing him speak one night and I thought he was going to speak on Japan, but he spoke on John 3:16: "For God so loved the world." He was the voice of conscience for the assemblies of Ulster: fearless in exposing what was wrong: prodding when things were slowing down; and forever stirring things up in a day of lethargy. The family, the world, the assemblies are the poorer for his passing."

ELLIS HARRISON

Ellis was the thirteenth child of a lapsed Catholic, but most of the family died before adulthood. Their father showed little interest in spiritual things until shortly before his death, but young Ellis was taken to a Gospel Hall by an older brother and sister while they were young. Ellis was saved at an early age and taken to an Independent Methodist Church by older members of the family. He was interested in spiritual things from a very early age, becoming a local preacher and Bible Class leader when he was seventeen. However he was not happy with the Methodist attitude to believers' baptism and eternal security. He was therefore baptised by immersion in Foster Street Gospel Hall in his native town of Warrington.

Shortly afterwards, being the invited preacher at a large Methodist Church, after his sermon he was handed a baby to christen. In spite of his youth Ellis explained to the congregation why he couldn't do it, and an old man had to be found who would. This kind of thing forced Ellis and his friends to consider their position, so Ellis and another brother, accompanied by the whole of the Bible Class, in number about two dozen, left to set up a new work. The only married couple in the group were Ellis' future in-laws. For a meeting-place they purchased a wooden hut, the Kerfoot Street Mission.

The group had little intention of being regarded as another meeting of "brethren", but following New Testament principles that's what they became. Former Methodist contacts continued to be invited to preach along with men like Alfred Mace, Russell Elliott, Willie Hagan, etc., but with the danger of unacceptable teaching from the former group they were eventually dropped. For all of his life Ellis spared no expense to get good Bible teaching for the assembly he was leading.

Other assemblies viewed the new group with suspicion, but they plodded on. Sacrificial giving enabled the young group to improve the hut. Jewellery was put into the offering box and hair was cut less often to save money, and indeed stopped being cut at all. Finally Hope Hall was opened in 1930 on the Bewsey Estate and after several meetings with the Foster Street brethren fellowship was arranged and Warrington had two New Testament assemblies.

The new assembly provided the lifework of E. H., as he was called. There is little doubt that it came before his shop, which was sacrificed for the assembly's sake. He did give a helping hand elsewhere, for instance helping Harry Brown of Warrington (who later went to Africa), to preach and establish an assembly or two in the Cotswolds. He worked with Garnet Thomas among the armed forces during the Second World War. He helped in the establishment of the Rest and Reception Room at Padgate R.A.F. Camp. This work reached thousands of young men, many of whom were also entertained in believers' homes like the Harrisons'. Evangelists like Arthur Greenwood preached at Padgate and he also conducted tent campaigns.

After the War E. H. had a vision of a Sunday School on another new estate and various brethren and sisters provided the teaching staff who conducted this in a Social Club. The children sometimes perched on beer barrels to listen to the gospel. Among visitors to this work was the late J. B. Watson. This developed into the assembly in Hebron Hall, Longford.

Ellis Harrison travelled fairly extensively ministering the Word in former days, but latterly he gave his undivided attention to Hope Hall. Everything received his undivided attention. Latterly he was quite unwell and elders' meetings were transferrred to the Harrison's home. Losing touch with reality he still seemed to have a grasp of spiritual things. Finally he had to enter hospital where in his confusion he preached to other patients and recited scripture to the staff. After all it had been his whole life.

A close friend of Ellis Harrison described him as "a man for all seasons". He was a born leader and did everything well-precentor, chairman, secretary, preacher, host. Under him Hope Hall became a landmark. Annually for many years evangelists were brought to conduct gospel campaigns. Regularly teaching brethren came for ministry. The annual conference could draw audiences of up to 400.

His brethren paid tribute to him in these words, "He never lost his concern for the spiritual wellbeing of those on Bewsey Estate surrounding Hope Hall. . . . Some men are remembered for their work in designing and building edifices like St. Paul's. E. H. watched nearly every brick go into the building of Hope Hall, but he will be remembered in the transformed lives of converts, in the building of Christian character ("that Christ may be formed in you" was his constant prayer), and in the continuance of assembly work in Warrington.

CONCLUSION

"The Quiet Majority"

THE UNSUNG HEROES OF THE CHURCH

The couple belong to that great company of unknown and unsung heroes of the church. It is a renowned company in which to have a place. You rub shoulders with those who, with bountiful blessings, founded the missionary church at Antioch. (Acts 11:19–21). We know where the messengers came from but we don't know their names.

Who founded the church in Rome? There is reason to believe the unknown commentator of the fourth century who suggested that the gospel reached the imperial city before any apostle arrived there. After all there were Romans in Jerusalem on that famous Pentecost day who heard the Gospel preached in the power of God's Spirit (Acts 2:10). Whoever they were, they all belong to the ranks of this great company of Christ's unknown servants.

Who preached the good news of salvation in Spain in the first century of the Christian era? There is insufficient historical evidence to be certain that the apostle Paul visited Spain even though he fully intended to do so. (Rom. 15:24–28). Who were those pioneer missionaries who took the Gospel across the sea to distant Spain?

The most plausible explanation for the very early evangelisation of Spain may be found in the constant movement between Rome and Spain, one of the most important provinces in the Empire at that time. Paul refers to the "saints" in Caesar's household. (cf. Phil. 4:22). There were thousands of men and

221

women employed in the imperial establishment. The term is wide enough to include slaves, servants and members of the civil service, whether in Rome or in the provinces, all employed in the service of the Emperor. Christian slaves, servants and diplomats of the imperial household, besides businessmen and ordinary travellers, may well have been the messengers who took the gospel with them to the Iberian Peninsula. A Christian was a Christian wherever he or she might be. It was not necessary to be a preacher in order to spread the gospel. It was the custom for early Christians to simply be involved with "telling the message ..." to others with whom they came into contact. (Acts 11:19). The men and women inovlved in the initial evangelisation of Spain belong to this great company of unknown servants of Christ. We thank God with all our hearts for those who are well known to us e.g., Paul, the apostle, untiring missionary and great theologian. We are encouraged by their faithful lives, by their willingness to sacrifice, and by their outstanding work. But we should always remember the many unknown followers of Christ, unknown in the earthly chronicles of church history, and, for that reason unknown to us. Undoubtedly they are all well known to God. For each of them, and also for each of us in our somewhat obscure service for God, the well-known statement still stands: "Your labour is not in vain in the Lord." (1 Cor. 15:58)

After writing a great deal about heroes of faith the writer to the Hebrews makes a concise reference to "... all these ..." (11:39) This important term would include the outstanding personalities of the Old Testament, and also the unnamed prophets of v. 32, the unknown women of v. 35, and the "others" of vs. 35–36. All these, the famous and the unknown, "... won a glowing testimony to their faith ..." (Phillips). Writing of faithful stewards, Paul states that "then shall every man have praise from God." (1 Cor. 4:5).

By their sheer numbers these unsung heroes constitute the quiet majority in the great cloud of witnesses that surround us today (Heb. 12:1). Men and women are illustrious servants in the eyes of God. Together with those who are well known they also encourage us to go on in the service of the Lord Jesus, "... on whom faith depends from start to finish ..." (Heb. 12:2 NEB).

J. R. Cochrane
in "Missions" magazine

INDEX

(of departed brethren mentioned in text)

	Page
AINSWORTH, G.	24–5
ASHBY, J.	6
BAEHR, C.	201
BARKER, H. P.	1, 192
BARKER, W.	192
BARTON, G.	63
BAVERSTOCK, G.	191
BENTALL BROS.	81
BERNARD, J.	105
BIFFEN, H.	1
BOYD, J. McC.	122
BROADBENT, E. H.	69
BROMLEY, E. B.	122
BROWN, J. H	5–6
BRYANT, F.	76
BUNTING, W.	106
BUTCHER, F.	71
CHURCHILL, T.	181
CLARE, W.	11
COOPER, R. W.	71
CRAWFORD, D.	191
CUFF, A.	133
CUNNINGHAM, Mr. & Mrs.	147
CURTIS, J.	158
DAWSON, J. C. M.	105
DUFF, J.	160
FEREDAY, W. W.	81
FISHER, S.	147
FISKE, Capt.	46, 111
GABRIEL, C.	44–6, 110
GEMMELL, J. K.	76
GILMORE, W.	116
GLEN, S.	191
GOODMAN BROS.	75
GRAY, J.	55
GREENWOOD, A.	218
GRIFFITHS, D.	68, 72–3
HALE, H.	191
HAY, T.	199
HEWITT, J.	200
HOCKING, A.	167
HODSON, J.	191
HOGG, C. F.	15
HOLT, T.	30
HORNE, P. J.	68, 124, 151
HOYTE, J.	101
JOHNSON, K. A.	77

	Page
KNOX, F.	115
LAIDLAW, R. A.	126
LAING, Sir J.	143, 160
LAMB, H. G.	109–110
LANG, G. H.	69
LEE, C.	134
LEWIS, W. R.	143
McALPINE, J.	59, 151
McCRACKEN, W.	106
McCULLOUGH, J.	106
McKNIGHT, J. H.	105
MALTZMAN, A.	70
MATTHEWS, Dr.	105
MOORE, S.	106
MORSE, A.	192
MOSCROP, M. R.	79
NICHOLAS, W.	191
PAYNE, W.	75
PETERKIN, A. C.	151
PICKERING, H.	55
PRESCOTT, J.	147
PUCKNELL, F. W.	77
REES, T. B.	55
ROGERS, E. W.	60, 77, 97
SCAMMELL, R.	122
SCOTT, J.	121
SCOTT, W.	181
SHNEIDROOK	69, 73
SHORT, Prof. R.	12
STEPHEN, J	12
STEWART, J.	105–6
ST. JOHN, H.	47, 60, 81
TATE, P.	192
THOMAS, G.	191
TILSLEY, C.	122, 191
VINE, W. E.	142–3, 181
VINES, R.	133
WALES, T.	59
WARD, D.	121–2
WATSON, J. B.	77, 82
WEBB, J.	122
WIDDISON, A.	192
WILLY, E.	46, 93
WYNCOLL, C.	6
YOELSON-TAFFIN, J.	90
ZENTLER, F.	11
ZINDER, R.	82

223